ARMED WITH SPIRIT

A FATHER'S ADVICE TO HIS SON IN THE ISRAELI ARMY
BASED ON THE WEEKLY TORAH PORTIONS

Thank you for your hospitality

RABBI SHALOM HAMMER

WITH A FOREWORD BY RABBI BEREL WEIN

gefen
publishing house
JERUSALEM • NEW YORK   Est. 1981

Scripture quotations are modified from *The Holy Scriptures According to
the Masoretic Text*, published by the Jewish Publication Society in 1917.

Cover Design:
Typesetting: Benjie Herskowitz

ISBN: 978-965-229-967-3
1 3 5 7 9 8 6 4 2

Gefen Publishing House Ltd.   Gefen Books
6 Hatzvi Street   140 Fieldcrest Ave
Jerusalem 94386, Israel   Edison, NJ 08837
972-2-538-0247   516-593-1234
orders@gefenpublishing.com   orders@gefenpublishing.com

www.gefenpublishing.com
Printed in Israel

Library of Congress Cataloging-in-Publication Data

Names: Hammer, Shalom, author.
Title: Armed with spirit : a father's advice to his son in the Israeli army
  based on the weekly Torah portions / by Shalom Hammer.
Description: Jerusalem ; Edison NJ : Gefen Publishing House Ltd., [2019]
Identifiers: LCCN 2018048358 | ISBN 9789652299673
Subjects: LCSH: Bible. Pentateuch — Commentaries. | Fasts and feasts
  — Judaism.
 | Fathers and sons — Israel.
Classification: LCC BS1225.53 .H3575 2019 | DDC 296.092/25694 — dc23
LC record available at https://lccn.loc.gov/2018048358

Dedicated in loving memory of
Dov Ber Ben Yitzchak HaLevi,
our family patriarch, a wise man
whose actions spoke louder than words.

He was a leader who touched many with his kindness
and generosity and gave of himself selflessly
to all in the community.

⸺⸙⸺

לכבוד
יעקב יחיאל בן שלום אברהם הלוי
ולכל חיילי צבא ההגנה לישראל
ילכו מחיל אל חיל יראה אל אלהים בציון
(תהלים פרק פד)

Sponsored in loving memory of our grandparents Samuel Velkes, Alf and Tilly Beerman, Yudel and Sylvia Katz and Saiah and Sarah Adelson.

— KIM AND LANCE KATZ

৩৫ ৯৯

Dedicated to all the brave men and women in Tzahal who are defending our country.

— TAMAR AND MARC LESNICK AND FAMILY

৩৫ ৯৯

Dedicated to the brave men and women who serve in the IDF and keep our homeland safe.

— SARAH AND MARTY KORNBLUM

৩৫ ৯৯

Dedicated to the memory of my dear loving parents Dovid and Suri Schwartz, *a"h*, both of whom were survivors of the Holocaust and both of whom never lost faith in Hashem. Their mission was to instill in their children, grandchildren, great grandchildren and great-great-grandchildren Torah values, chesed, and a love for Jews everywhere. שלי שלכם.

And in memory of my dear loving father, Irwin (Yisroel Eizig) Friedman, who did not allow the horrors of the Holocaust to strip him of his humanity and became a loving husband, father, grandfather, great-grandfather and a gentleman to all.

— MENDY AND LYNN (NÉE FRIEDMAN) SCHWARTZ, ATLANTIC CITY, NJ

৩৫ ৯৯

In memory of my dad, Stewart Harris, who loved the State of Israel and the young men and women who defend it on a daily basis. He also loved and was proud of Rabbi Hammer despite the countless teenager incidents that led to his ouster from our home.
— Your Friend **DAVID HARRIS**

֎ ֎֎

Dedicated to our precious children, Leo, Maya, and Noa. May our Jewish nation serve as inspiration for you always.
— With love, **TALYA AND MICHAEL BACHMANN**

֎ ֎֎

לזכר נשמות הורינו היקרים
אברהם משה בן הרב שלמה זאלי ז"ל וגוטקה טובה בת רב אברהם דוד ע"ה
למשפחת ביננפלד
יהודה לייב בן אהרון זאב ז"ל וחוה מינה בת יצחק אייזיק ע"ה
למשפחת יוסדן
— מוקדש ע"י ר' מנחם שמואל והדסה ביננפלד

֎ ֎֎

In honor of our children Tehilla, Ely, Daniella, Ariella, AB, Shuki H., Shuki K. and Miri, who have served, currently serve, and will be serving in the IDF. No words can express the deep love and pride we have for you all.
ובזכות שירותכם לעם ישראל ולארצו, הקב"ה ימלא את משאלות
לבכם לטובה
— Love always, **ABBA REUVEN AND IMA ELKE**

֎ ֎֎

Approbation from Rabbi Yosef Tzvi Rimon

יוסף צבי רימון

רבה של אלון שבות דרום
ראש הישיבה, ראש בתי המדרש
ורב המרכז האקדמי לב
ונשיא סולמות

רחוב קבוצת אברהם 10
אלון שבות 9043300
משרד: 02-9933644
נייד: 052-5456060
פקס: 153-2-9933644
rimonim613@gmail.com

I was mesmerized reading this book, which Rabbi Shalom Hammer wrote during the course of his son's army service, for a number of reasons. First, the very fact that a father invests so much time and concern writing to his son daily to offer him advice and a source of strength should itself be an inspiration to all of us regarding parental investment in a child. Second, the wide array of topics within the letters and conversations are extremely pertinent and significant to Jewish foundations, such as how to relate to our fellow man, the importance of keeping mitzvot even within time constraints, wearing tzitzit and tefillin, taking time to learn a minimum of Torah every day, being wary of one's speech, and of course the importance of sacrificing one's personal interests for the sake of a nation.

In addition Rabbi Hammer reveals through this correspondence the importance of serving in Tzahal and recognizing the redemption evolving in front of our eyes and the wondrous opportunity we have to live in Eretz Yisrael.

I get calls from *chayalim* daily, and while I sense their strength and resilience, I also sense their struggle. Serving in Tzahal can be a challenge to religious commitments, but it can also be inspiring. One of the factors that can help a *chayal*'s observance during his service is the spiritual and ideological support of a parent. Rabbi Hammer is an outstanding model for parents; I encourage all parents in this situation to follow his example and nurture meaningful connections with your children particularly during their army service.

Aside from the halachic and ideological sources and ideas that Rabbi Hammer imparts, there are also particularly moving segments in the book, such as the advice he offers his son Yakov before Yom Kippur.

I want to extend a *berachah* to Rabbi Hammer that he should continue to be a source of strength for Torat Am Yisrael, and his book should inspire *chayalim* and parents who are privileged to have children serving in Tzahal.

Blessings
Rabbi Yosef Tzvi Rimon, Alon Shvut

מכתב ברכה לספר צבא עם רוח

יוסף צבי רימון

רבה של אלון שבות דרום
ראש הישיבה, ראש בתי המדרש
ורב המרכז האקדמי לב
נשיא סולמות

רחוב קבוצת אברהם 10
אלון שבות 9043300

משרד: 9933644-02
נייד: 5456060-052
פקס: 9933644-153-2

rimonim613@gmail.com

בס"ד, כ"ה בניסן ה'תשע"ט

התפעלתי מאוד מספרו של הרב שלום המר, שכתב לבנו במהלך שירותו הצבאי. ומדוע התפעלתי? ראשית, מעצם העובדה שאב משקיע כל כך הרבה בבנו, וכותב לו בכל יום מכתב חיזוק. דבר זה הוא דגם ומסר לכולם, עד כמה צריכים ההורים להשקיע בילדיהם.

שנית, מהכתיבה המשמעותית בנושאים מגוונים כל כך: דברים משמעותיים על חשיבות בין אדם לחבירו; על החשיבות לשמור על דביקות במצוות גם כאשר אין הרבה זמן; ענייני הנחת תפילין; מצוות ציצית; לימוד מינימים של תורה; על הזהירות להישמר מהשתתפות בשיח לא ראוי; על הצורך שיש לעתים להקריב התקדמות אישית כדי לקדם אחרים או לעסוק בצרכי העם.

פרט לכך, ניתן לראות דברים רבים על החשיבות של שירות בצה"ל, ועל ההתרגשות מהגאולה שבה אנו זוכים להיות כיום, בשובו של עם ישראל לארץ ישראל.

חיילים רבים מתקשרים אלי מידי יום ביומו. אני חש את העוצמה שלהם אך גם את הקשיים המיוחדים. תקופת הצבא יכולה להיות תקופה שיש בה ירידה רוחנית, אולם, יכולה להיות גם תקופה עם עליה רוחנית. אחד הדברים שיכולים לסייע לכך הוא התמיכה הרוחנית של ההורים. הדגם שמציב הרב המר בספרו הוא דגם חשוב מאוד, ואני מחזק את ההורים ללכת בעקבותיו, וליצור נתיבים לחיבור רוחני מיוחד עם ילדיהם, דווקא בשלב זה של השירות הצבאי.

בתוך הקטעים ההלכתיים והמחשבתיים, יש גם קטעים מרגשים במיוחד, כמו החיזוק שנותן הרב המר לבנו יעקב לקראת יום הכיפורים.

אני מברך את הרב המר שליט"א שיזכה להמשיך להגדיל תורה ולהאדירה, ספרו זה יחזק חיילים רבים והורים רבים שזכו בכך שבנם משרת בצבא.

ברכת ה' עליכם,

יוסף צבי רימון

Approbation from Rabbanit Shani Taragin

Rabbi Hammer's correspondence with his son resembles an ongoing *chavruta* through the *parashiyot* and *moadim* (festivals) of the year. The reader is drawn into the discussion, marveling at the love of Am Yisrael, Eretz Yisrael, and Torat Yisrael shared between father and son. Their voices echo questions of the past and simultaneously resonate with contemporary queries and challenges. Each letter amplifies the messages of our Torat Chayim, strengthening and inspiring Yakov together with all our sons to face a reality we have not encountered for nearly two thousand years – an Israeli army defending the State of Israel! How obvious then to garner strength from words of Torah as they reverberate louder than ever with the renewed fulfillment of patriarchal promises and covenantal commitment.

Some letters brought tears to my eyes, recounting conversations I have had with my own sons. More overwhelming, however, than the accompanying anxiety that every parent feels with children in the army is the sense of tremendous pride felt in every correspondence recorded: pride in his son, pride in every son, pride in our nation, our land, and our rich Torah tradition, offering *chizuk* to parents and children, from generation to generation.

Armed with Spirit aptly depicts the poignant and imperative messages for the contemporary *chayal/chayelet* seeking not only to maintain religious identity while serving in the army, but to spiritually grow and develop through the experience as well. Rabbi Hammer "arms" and provides inspirational messages for the soldiers, while symbiotically learning and sharing *divrei Torah* with a renewed perspective, invigorating the parent/teacher with tools of spirit as he learns with and from his son. "Not by might, nor by power, but by My spirit," encourages Zechariah (4:6) during the time of Shivat Tzion. Thank you, Rabbi Hammer, for transforming these words of prophecy to fulfillment through your timely and thought-provoking messages of Torah learning and living!

Rabbanit Shani Taragin, Alon Shvut

CONTENTS

FOREWORD

Part of daily life in Israel is the reality that our young men and women serve in the Israel Defense Forces, or as we know it, Tzahal.[1] This is an emotional and challenging experience, both for the family and the young person in the army. It is especially challenging for religious families and observant young people because the nature of army life, war, and violence is not always conducive to Torah study and Torah values. Nevertheless, the circumstances in which we live make it impossible for Israel to exist without well-trained armed forces. These young and impressionable soldiers, and their families, need strength and encouragement, particularly in spiritual and Torah matters.

This book records the correspondence between a father and a son during the years the son was serving in the Israel Defense Forces. It is a personal and insightful record of a family relationship, but in a broader sense, it represents the thousands of families and young people who have found themselves in these challenging circumstances.

How is one to view army life? How is one to retain religious values, strength of character, and piety of behavior in an environment that is not necessarily conducive to such aspirations? What, if any, ideas can be communicated to maintain and strengthen the family relationship of a young man who is now in a different environment: not living at home and on his own, so to speak, even though subject to army rules? All of these questions are reflected in this very personal, well-written, and inspirational book. It tells the story of a father and son, and it tells the story of generations here in Eretz Yisrael (the Land of Israel). It gives us a view into the mind and soul of the state, its young people, and those families that value Torah greatly and attempt to communicate that message to the next generation as well.

---

1   Tzva Hahaganah l'Yisrael, literally "Israel Defense Forces."

XIII

Rabbi Shalom Hammer, a renowned lecturer, speaker, and Torah scholar, has recorded his correspondence with his son during the years the young man served as a combat soldier in Tzahal. The book is honest and inspirational. It offers the reader a true sense of life in Israel and how it impacts people and families. I can recommend this book to all Jews, wherever they may live, because within it breathes the Jewish spirit and the heart and mind of the Jewish generation in which we live.

Rabbi Hammer has illuminated the innermost feelings of family and of the state, combined with knowledge, faith, and the inspiration of Torah. May the Lord bless him and his family and all of the young men and women who sacrifice so much to preserve the miracle of our time, the State of Israel.

Rabbi Berel Wein

PREFACE

Many of us are aware how difficult it is physically to train as a combat soldier and serve in the IDF; but how many know of the spiritual challenges that come with serving in Tzahal? Observant young men and women encounter many challenges while serving in the army. The Israeli army purports to be a halachically observant institution, but the majority of *chayalim* (soldiers) who serve in Tzahal are secular. Suddenly, the insular world of young and impressionable observant eighteen-year-olds clashes with an unrestricted secular world and an irreligious atmosphere they are not accustomed to. As a lecturer in the IDF and a teacher for many pre-military academies, I am aware of the encounters that these youngsters will inevitably face in the army, and so when it was time for our older son Yakov to enlist, I was prepared for his sake and for my own.

Yakov is an observant young man who spent two years in Atzmona, a popular religious pre-military academy. He drafted as a combat soldier for the Nahal Brigade Battalion 50 and reached the rank of *samal* (staff sergeant). The Nahal Brigade consists of young men who, prior to their army service, serve a year or two of national service or, as in Yakov's case, spend two years studying Torah in a pre-military academy.

The majority of the young men in Battalion 50 are nonobservant members of the secular Shomer Hatzair kibbutz movement. The groups serving in this battalion consist of what are known as *garinim* (seed) groups. Yakov's *garin* comprised nine observant friends who drafted together with 121 secular soldiers from various kibbutzim because they wanted to fulfill a *kiddush Hashem* among secular Jews and unify under the banner of Tzahal.

Army service in the IDF was a minimum of thirty-two months at the time, and while we were supportive of Yakov and where he chose to serve, I knew there were religious challenges to come. From the very first day of his service, I promised him, and perhaps more so myself, that every day I would send him a *dvar Torah* (a word on the weekly Torah portion or *parashah*) message on his WhatsApp. Frankly, I was not sure whether he would read them every day, but I wanted him to know that they were available if he was looking for something inspirational. It is for this reason that I chose different *divrei Torah* every day from varied sources, with the intention of finding something from that week's *parashah* that related to his serving in the Israeli army as an observant soldier. From my perspective, I felt that if these *divrei Torah* were with him on a daily basis, there was a better chance that Yakov would be safe and secure in more ways than one. Finally, these *divrei Torah* were a means of remaining connected with my son, and although we were physically apart, the Torah would keep us together. I was convinced that I was doing both of us a favor, but what became clear was that I had underestimated the impact of our interaction.

Yakov read the *divrei Torah*. What evolved were conversations and exchanges between us that were meaningful and insightful, succinct as they were, due to time constraints on both sides and limited access to the phone on his side. Yakov is generally a complacent and affable young man – he would certainly not be described as a conversationalist – and yet our conversations taught me that he was far more reflective than I had realized. At times this correspondence even revealed to me that he is more concerned regarding his commitment to observance than he would have me know, and so our communication was as insightful to me as I hoped it would be for him, which is what inspired me to gather our letters together into a book for the benefit of others.

This book was compiled with a number of objectives in mind:

- I want to give people an inside glimpse of the Israeli army from a religious point of view.
- I want other parents to appreciate what Israeli parents go through as they deliver their children (which is exactly what

they are when they begin their service) to the army, burdening them with the awesome and overwhelming responsibility of preserving the Jewish world.

- I want to share with you *divrei Torah* that I shared with my son, the soldier, to inspire him to remain loyal to what is vital to Jewish existence. I certainly hope they will inspire you to do the same, regardless of the circumstances in which you find yourself.

- I want the reader to appreciate these outstanding individuals, *chayalei Tzahal*, who represent the crème de la crème of Am Yisrael today as they approach their service with fervor, sincerity, and devotion.

These WhatsApp *divrei Torah* spanned a period of three years. We could not print all of the material in one book; therefore, the subject matter was chosen carefully, based on what I felt would resonate with the theme and objectives delineated above. Given that soldiers are not called to enlist en masse on a specific day and month, and certainly not in accordance with the annual Torah reading cycle, our letters have been presented from the time of Yakov's enlistment through to the end of his service, following the *parashiyot* as the weeks and years progressed. The book is based on the original conversations and incorporates many original messages, but has been added to and edited for publication. I have tried to keep the format as true to our conversations as possible: a *dvar Torah* from me, followed, in most cases, by Yakov's response.

Toward the end of the book I have included excerpts from my lectures to IDF soldiers, as well as reflections, anecdotes, and stories that convey the ideals of Zionism, religion, Eretz Yisrael (the Land of Israel), and Am Yisrael (the Jewish people), as they relate to Tzahal.

LETTERS TO MY SON

Basic Training:
Deuteronomy

On average basic training is three and a half months for combat soldiers. During this time the main focus is discipline; training soldiers to follow the rules of Tzahal and integrating soldiers into the system. It is particularly challenging for the new recruits who are unaccustomed to following strict procedures and restrictions. I tried to offer words of encouragement in my divrei Torah as much as possible.

Vaetchanan

August 2, 2015

Yakov,

Reflecting upon your just having been drafted to Tzahal, I started to think about what I could say to you on the beginning of a new, exciting, but most challenging chapter in your life. I thought of the following insight that I wanted to share with you: Parashat Vaetchanan (which we read yesterday) begins with Moshe beseeching Hashem (God; literally, "the Name") to allow him entry to Eretz Yisrael, something he anticipated his entire life, but there is something outstanding within his request: "Let me now cross and see the good land that is on the other side of the Jordan..."[2]

Moshe desires not only to cross the Jordan to Israel, but he also wishes to "see the good land," as he describes it. Israel is a land that is subject to interpretation. Some look at the land and see only trial and tribulation, challenge, and despair. Yet there are others who look at the land and see hope and promise, regardless of the struggles; they look at the land and they see "good"; it is all a matter of perspective.

You are familiar with the story I often tell how I once turned to an Israeli friend of mine who had never left Eretz Yisrael and remarked to him that sometimes I appreciated leaving this land and going to a country such as the United States in the Diaspora where there's plenty of elbow room, people are more patient and less anxious and even drive normally. I concluded by saying, "Sometimes I find that this country is too small for me." He in turn looked at me and without hesitation retorted, "Really? Sometimes I find that I am too small for this country." It all boils down to perspective.

_____

2   Deuteronomy 3:25.

5

You are starting basic training in the Israeli army, and you will no doubt experience hardships and challenges, but it would serve you well to remember that our great military and spiritual teacher Moshe never set foot on the land that you now protect. My dear son, you now have the privilege to serve as protector of the Jewish people, to demonstrate to others the holiness and greatness that our land provides for its people, and may it be the will of Hashem that your perception consistently encourages you to "see the good land."

With love and admiration,

Abba

August 3, 2015

Good morning, Yakov.

The Shabbat following the ninth of Av is referred to as Shabbat Nachamu, which we just experienced two days ago. *L'nachem* in Hebrew is "to find comfort"; we attempt to comfort ourselves following our three-week period of mourning over the destruction of the Batei Hamikdash (the two Holy Temples). Parashat Vaetchanan is consistently read on Shabbat Nachamu as well. What is the intrinsic connection between *nechamah* (comfort) and Vaetchanan?

On the ninth of Av, one is not allowed to immerse in Torah study because it initiates true happiness. However, following the ninth of Av and the state of sorrow we found ourselves in for the three weeks prior, we are encouraged to slowly return to a state of bliss. Therefore, immediately following the ninth of Av, the *parashah* of Vaetchanan is read; this is the *parashah* that describes Am Yisrael's acceptance of the Torah at Har Sinai, which is the most authentic source of happiness.

There are many people who are infatuated with pleasing themselves, but they may never experience happiness. Happiness is the result of meaning, purpose, and fulfillment, and the greatest facilitator of such aspirations is the Torah itself. It is for this reason that immediately following the three weeks, we turn to our greatest source of *nechamah*, a comfort that can only be provided by accepting the Torah and what it stands for. This allows us the comfort of knowing how to expedite our reconstruction and the comfort of knowing that we can experience meaningful purpose and fulfillment in this world.

Serving in Tzahal is the greatest means of dedication to the Jewish world today. Serving in Tzahal with a kippah (yarmulke) on your head and tzitzit strapped around your body is the greatest way to demonstrate that you are privileged and feel happy to make that commitment.

May your service bring you happiness, and may your continued commitment to our source of happiness bring comfort to our entire nation.

Abba

Ekev

August 4, 2015

Good evening, Yakov.

Parashat Ekev begins, "This shall be [the reward] when you hearken to these ordinances."[3] The Torah contains ordinances and statutes, and generally speaking, the difference between them is that we understand the logic behind the ordinances, while the statutes are not always as comprehensible and are therefore more difficult to submit to.

The *Meshech Chochmah* explains that here the Torah refers only to the ordinances and makes no mention of the statutes, even though they were expected to execute both, because Bnei Yisrael were so subservient to Hashem at this juncture that they were willing to perform the statutes wholeheartedly as if they were ordinances.

As you go through your basic training and service, there will be many things expected of you and services you will have to render that may not make sense, particularly at the time when you have to implement them; yet as a *chayal*, you are expected to follow orders regardless of your limited understanding of them. I hope and pray that you will fulfill these "statutes" unconditionally as a result of understanding the nature of your commitment to your people and to your land.

Abba

▶ *Thank you for your encouragement and blessings. You are probably right, although I have not experienced near enough in the army yet to confirm your concern. Having said that, I am confident that the commitment you and Mommy have shown me at home will be helpful, and I too hope and pray it will carry over to my service in the army.*

---

3 Deuteronomy 7:12.

August 5, 2015

Yakov,

One of the things that Hashem warns the Jewish people about in this week's *parashah* is "V'hayah [it shall be] that if you forget Hashem, your God, and go after the gods of others...I will testify against you today that you will surely perish."[4]

The Radziner Rebbe explains that the word used to introduce this warning is *v'hayah*, which in biblical terminology usually refers to a context of being happy, as in the case of the second portion of the Shema prayer, which also appears in this Torah portion: "*V'hayah* [it shall be] if you listen to My commandments...then I shall provide rain for your Land..."[5] Making the association between "*v'hayah*" and the warning not to forget Hashem, the Radziner explains that if a person is not happy, he is liable to forget Hashem; therefore one is required not only to fulfill the mitzvot, but also to do so with happiness.

This is substantiated in the Talmud, which says, "The divine spirit cannot reside in a place of sadness, but only in a place where there is happiness."[6]

My dear son, I know that yesterday it was exceedingly hot, and you must have had a very tough day as you began your basic training; remember that the divine spirit of Hashem dwells in places that are happy. Try to adopt positive perspectives by reminding yourself of the importance of what you are doing and that will serve as a source of happiness which in turn will cause Hashem's spirit to reside around you.

---

4   Deuteronomy 8:9.
5   Deuteronomy 11:13–14.
6   Babylonian Talmud, *Pesachim* 117a.

August 6, 2015

Yakov,

The Torah encourages the Jewish people to conquer Eretz Yisrael by reminding them of the special relationship they share with Hashem: "You shall not fear them! You shall remember what Hashem, your God, did to Pharaoh and to all of Egypt. The great tests that your eyes saw, and the signs, the wonders."[7]

Yet less than two chapters later the Jewish people are told: "Not because of your righteousness or the uprightness of your heart do you go in to possess their land, but because of the wickedness of these nations does the Lord, your God, drive them away from before you,"[8] clearly indicating that their conquest of Eretz Yisrael has nothing to do with their relationship with Hashem or with their merit, but rather the other nations' wickedness.

Perhaps the Torah is offering us a formula for success. On the one hand, Hashem expects us to remember His Divine Presence, but we are also compelled to understand that our salvation is in our hands and it should not result from the wickedness of our enemies but should emerge ideally from our good deeds and righteousness. This formula is essential during your service in the army: always remain faithful to your belief in Hashem, but look for ways to enhance that faith by way of your actions and good deeds. This balance will provide you with success.

With love and admiration,

Abba

---

7   Deuteronomy 7:18, 19.
8   Deuteronomy 9:5.

August 7, 2015

Yakov,

The Torah uses the word *ekev* (heel) to introduce the *berachot* and reward Am Yisrael will receive if they "hearken to these ordinances"[9] of Hashem; this usage is peculiar. One can explain the word literally: committing to the mitzvot begins with *ekev*, as it requires picking up one's heel and moving one's legs in order to perform the mitzvot themselves.

The Kotzker Rebbe refers to the end of the verse, which says, "The Lord, your God, will keep with you the covenant and the mercy that He swore to your forefathers"[10]. This "covenant" is the assurance Hashem gave to our forefathers that their descendants, Am Yisrael, would inherit Eretz Yisrael. Therefore, the entire context of the beginning of the *parashah* refers to one specific mitzvah, that of inheriting and settling Eretz Yisrael.

Ekev – to walk and patrol Eretz Yisrael for the sake of inheriting and conquering it – undoubtedly poses many challenges, as we have witnessed in our past and continue to experience today, as you will learn to appreciate during your service in Tzahal. Yet if we "hearken to these ordinances" of Hashem, we will succeed in our endeavor and be privy to the greatest reward of all: to secure and settle our land.

While I will miss you over Shabbat, it is comforting to know that you have embraced the mission of *ekev*. While your service in the army may obstruct you from fulfilling Shabbat in its full halachic context, remember that during all your patrols, while you are guarding and running to secure a post, you consistently fulfill with your *ekev* the essential mitzvah of ensuring that all the Jewish people can walk in the land of our ancestors.

Shabbat shalom.

---

9 Deuteronomy 7:12.
10 Deuteronomy 7:12.

▶ *Much appreciated, Abba. I remember you used to tell us on Yom Ha'atzmaut that Rav Kook would celebrate by finding a new daled amot (four handbreadths) to walk in Eretz Yisrael because the Gemara establishes that each new daled amot that one walks in Eretz Yisrael is a new mitzvah. This certainly applies to what you are suggesting regarding Parashat Ekev. While I won't be resting much over Shabbat, I will try to remember that I am fulfilling a mitzvah wherever I walk.*

    Shabbat shalom.

Reeh

August 11, 2015

In Parshat Reeh the Torah instructs how to deal with an Ir Hanidachat, a city in Israel which succumbs to idolatry, saying, "You shall gather all its spoils to the midst of the open square, and you shall burn with fire the city and all its spoils, every bit of it, to the Lord your God, and it shall be a heap forever; it shall not be rebuilt. And there shall cleave no part of the banned property to your hand, so that the Lord will turn from the fierceness of His anger, and show you mercy and have compassion on you and multiply you, as He swore to your forefathers…"[11]

Why does Hashem promise to "show you mercy and have compassion on you" in the midst of the instructions regarding what to do with this city of idolatry? This seems to be out of context.

The Ohr Hachayim explains that when one is involved in a mission of destruction, even if it is fulfilling the word of Hashem, it can cause a person to grow insensitive and even to become cruel. Therefore specifically at a time when Am Yisrael are involved in destroying a city into an "heap forever," Hashem says that He will "show you mercy and have compassion on you and multiply you" in order to remind His people that we must show compassion to mankind and remember that ultimately our task in the world is to be constructive and not destructive.

While a *chayal* must fulfill his mission, which can often involve expectations of destruction, we as a Jewish army must always remember that we do so for the sake of constructing mankind and civilization. We must always have in mind the importance of being compassionate and at times sympathetic even toward the likes of our enemies, as difficult as that might seem.

---

11   Deuteronomy 13:17–18.

Shoftim

August 16, 2015

Yakov,

This week's *parashah* begins with the directive "Judges and officers shall you appoint in all your cities – which the Lord, your God, gives you – tribe by tribe."[12]

Perhaps the Torah is not only directing us to appoint judges and officers, but also that they should be concerned with those things "which the Lord, your God, gives you." The only people equipped to lead Am Yisrael properly are those genuinely concerned with Hashem's laws.

The "judges and officers" today are our soldiers in Tzahal, and the key to their success is protecting that "which the Lord, your God, gives you."

Abba

▸ *Thank you, Abba, but we also have to remember that without those who sit and learn the Torah, we would not know the intrinsic value of that "which the Lord, your God, gives you." This is precisely why both the philosophical study and the practical fulfillment of the Torah must coexist, as I am sure you appreciate.*

Yes, well said; it brings to mind a number of articles written by Rav Aharon Lichtenstein, of blessed memory, which I often refer to and we have even discussed in passing. One is an article in the book *By His Light* in which he discusses centrist Orthodoxy, as opposed to what he labels "the Right" or what we refer to as "*charedim*." He says:

There are times when one must compromise, and this itself is an issue between us and the Right: How are we going to gauge the

---

12 Deuteronomy 16:18.

qualitative as opposed to the quantitative element? They are the champions of the qualitative, *shemen zayit zakh* [pure olive oil]…. We have a much greater commitment to the quantitative element, to reaching large segments of the community, even if we only reach them partially and the accomplishments are limited.

Even if we must, in a certain sense compromise, it cannot be out of default. I remember years back reading a very perceptive remark of the Lubavitcher Rebbe; he said, "The problem with the Conservatives is not that they compromise – it is that they make a principle out of compromise." We cannot, God forbid, make a principle out of compromise, nor can we lapse into it by default. But if we are to avoid lapsing, then that passionate commitment must be kept burning. It is only when we can attain that passionate commitment that Centrism as a vibrant and legitimate spiritual force can be attained.[13]

There is another article that Rav Lichtenstein wrote in *Leaves of Faith* which I also have brought to your attention in which he discusses the ideology of Hesder. In it he shares your sympathies as well:

When the Mishnah states, …"If there is no flour, there is no Torah; if there is no Torah, there is no flour," it hardly means that both are equally important. What it does mean is that both are, in fact, equally necessary, although, axiologically and teleologically, flour exists for the sake of Torah, and not vice versa.[14]

Anyway, I think we are both on the same page, just emphasizing different viewpoints. We can certainly discuss more when we are together again.

---

13   Rabbi Aharon Lichtenstein, *By His Light: Character and Values in the Service of God*, adapted by Rabbi Reuven Ziegler (Jerusalem: Ktav, 2003), 244–45. Used by permission of Rabbi Reuven Ziegler.

14   Rabbi Aharon Lichtenstein, "The Ideology of Hesder," *Leaves of Faith*, vol. 1, *The World of Jewish Learning* (Jerusalem: Ktav, 2003), 137.

August 20, 2015

Good evening, Yakov.

Bnei Yisrael is told to appoint for itself "judges and officers."[15] Immediately following this instruction, the Torah warns not to plant a tree used for idolatry and not to erect a stone pillar, even for the sake of offerings to Hashem.

What is the connection between the positive instruction and the prohibitive ones?

I came across a nice insight.

Judges and officers are the leaders of a society; perhaps the Torah wants us to appreciate great leaderships. A stone pillar does not move from its place, while a tree sways to and fro and remains rooted in the ground. On the one hand, a leader should show flexibility as a tree sways, but at the same time he should not compromise his beliefs and must remain faithful to his foundation, firm like a stone. This lesson offers a key for success in the army and life in general. You need to know how and when to be flexible with people and their demands, but also when to stand firm on your principles of faith.

You serve in a unit in which the majority of your comrades are not observant. No question it is important to befriend them and show understanding and tolerance (otherwise your service will be a very lonely one), but it is just as important to be loyal to your observance; this is the only way to ensure that you will be both liked and respected.

▶ *I understand what you are saying regarding balance in life, and I agree with that, but I also detect a sense of concern. I want to assure you I am very comfortable with my fellow soldiers, and we are even becoming good friends. The army is all about comradeship, and naturally we are all cementing a strong rapport with one*

---

15   Deuteronomy 16:18.

another, observant and nonobservant alike. Having said that, please be confident in the upbringing I received from you and the tradition that has been a significant part of my life for some years now. This is also why I went to learn in the mechinah *(preparation academy) for two years prior to going into the army: to strengthen my foundations of faith and learn how to handle conflicts and differences with nonobservant soldiers.*

I admire your ability to communicate your mindset. While I cannot promise I will succeed, I will try my best to respect your feelings. It is difficult for children to appreciate and understand that a parent has a need to say something and offer direction. In fact, the only time I think a child appreciates and understands this is when they themselves become parents as well. It is also important for me to gain perspective on the fact that you are a *chayal Tzahal* and that at a young age you are forced to grow up so quickly and confront reality, which often can be biting. This too is difficult for a parent to do, but I understand where it can be a point of frustration for you as well, and I will try to be more sensitive to that. You are blessed to have the opportunity to learn from these experiences, and we are blessed that we are learning from them as well.

▸ *Don't get down on yourself, Abba. I appreciate your direction (sometimes...), but I just don't want you to be overprotective. I suppose I would also appreciate your being more confident in who I am - in my ability to make decisions and mistakes on my own and hopefully learn from them and certainly deal with them.*

Ki Teitze

August 24, 2015

Good evening, Yakov.

I am sure that you are familiar with the fact that the last mitzvah in Parashat Ki Teitze is our obligation to remember what Amalek did to us in their attempt to destroy our nation by attacking us when we were most vulnerable upon our Exodus from Egypt, "Remember what Amalek did to you on the way as you came forth out of Egypt."[16]

The mitzvah preceding this one is the directive by which the Torah instructs us to be honest in business, as it says, "A perfect and honest weight shall you have, a perfect and honest measure shall you have, that your days may be long upon the land that the Lord your God gives you."[17]

Rabbi Naftali Zvi Yehuda Berlin (the Netziv) explains that the Torah connects these two mitzvot to teach us the importance of living a life of honesty and integrity and that if one does not, it will inevitably lead to destruction much like Amalek's attempts to destroy the Jewish nation. We must always try to behave honestly and sincerely both as individuals and as a nation, and serving in Tzahal is probably the greatest means of expressing devotion and sincerity on behalf of Am Yisrael in today's Jewish world.

---

16 Deuteronomy 25:17.
17 Deuteronomy 25:15.

Tekes Hashba'ah – Swearing-in Ceremony

This ceremony is meant to infuse the soldiers with a sense of belonging and pride as each soldier is sworn in to his service and receives his gun and a Bible from the commanding officer. Families of the soldiers come to watch with pride as their children are officially sworn in as soldiers. The ceremony is usually held on a Thursday, and at the end most soldiers are granted a furlough to go home with their families and enjoy Shabbat in the comfort of their homes.

August 27, 2015

Yakov,
Today is your swearing-in ceremony, and I am sure you are excited. We are proud of you. Please take a moment to read this en route to the ceremony.

Shiluach haken is the mitzvah to send a *ken* (mother bird) away before taking its eggs from its nest. The Torah uses a double directive when defining the mitzvah: "*shaleach teshalach*" (you shall surely send [the mother away]).[18]

One who performs this mitzvah is assured "that it may be well with you and that you may prolong your days."[19] What is so special about this particular mitzvah?

The Avnei Nezer explains that selfishness is the main source of sin. A person who wants the eggs of a bird is hungry and interested in satiating his appetite. When he sends the mother bird away prior to taking its eggs, he demonstrates concern and sensitivity toward the mother bird prior to satisfying his own needs, an act of sincerity and unselfishness. Therefore, one who performs this mitzvah is assured to "prolong his days" because his selflessness represents the means of ridding the world of sin.

Perhaps this explains the use of a double directive; the Torah wants us not only to fulfill *shaleach*, sending the mother away, but to also recognize that in so doing, we purge ourselves of selfish motives.

As a soldier in Tzahal, you are a *shaliach*; you have been sent to exemplify someone prepared to think of others before yourself.

Abba

► *Abba, I want you to know that I read your* divrei Torah. *I don't always have time to get back to you, and sometimes don't even have time to read them on the same day, but eventually I read them and appreciate them. What you say regarding a* shaliach *is very true and very meaningful. One of the human characteristics that we naturally try to combat is selfishness; I think people particularly in our day have a tendency to become self-centered and*

18   Deuteronomy 22:7.
19   Ibid.

think of themselves without reflecting enough on others. There is no doubt that our role as chayalim *automatically encourages us to prioritize others before ourselves and to think collectively as a nation and a people, as opposed to focusing on our own personal needs. It is really a blessing to have these attitudes automatically inculcated and to be presented with an opportunity to place others before myself.*

I look forward to seeing you guys at the ceremony and thank you and Mommy for teaching me to be proud to serve my country and people.

Ki Tavo

September 4, 2015

Yakov,

As the Torah clarifies the mitzvah of *bikurim*, Hashem reminds Am Yisrael to adhere to the mitzvot, saying, "This day, the Lord your God commands you to do these statutes and ordinances.... You have caused the Lord to declare Himself your God, and to walk in His ways."[20]

What does the Torah mean by saying that the Jewish people "caused the Lord to say"? Is it not more appropriate to say, "You said today that Hashem will be a God for you, and [you will] walk in His ways"?

The Ibn Ezra explains that this verse is the beginning of the *berachot* described in the *parashah*, and the most exceptional *berachah* for us to receive is when we adhere to Hashem's word so much that He Himself declares He is our God. When we adhere to the mitzvot, we "cause Hashem" to proudly declare that He will be a God for us.

You must have had a very difficult week but, Baruch Hashem, Shabbat has arrived. Shabbat allows us to reflect on Hashem and the world He created. You can reflect upon all the mitzvot you fulfilled this past week – mitzvot that are so crucial that they "cause Hashem to say": "I am proud of My soldiers who protect My people."

This is the greatest praise one can receive.

Baruch Hashem, you have been privileged to facilitate Hashem's Presence among you through your service. On Shabbat, you will have more opportunities to dwell in Hashem's Presence: "For the Lord, your God, walks in the midst of your camp to deliver you and to give up your enemies before you; therefore shall your camp be holy."[21]

---

20   Deuteronomy 26:16, 17.
21   Deuteronomy 23:15.

We miss you and wish you all Shabbat shalom.
With love and admiration,
Abba

▶ *Thanks. You often speak about the reason the Torah exempts certain people from serving in the army. One who builds a new home or plants a new vineyard and a newlywed are all exempt, and you always explain that all three of these people are involved in personal endeavors and investments (a home, a turf, and a family), and at the moment they are incapable of thinking in national terms. A chayal must be able to see the entire Jewish people and nation as one large family and the entire Land of Israel as a country that belongs to the entire people. Only someone who is capable of thinking in "national terms" is worthy of serving in the Jewish army. Shabbat is family time, and I will miss you guys, but I understand that as a chayal my "family" is more comprehensive, as it should be, and I appreciate the privilege to serve my family as well. Quite frankly, I am looking forward to sleeping.*
   Shabbat shalom.

Nitzavim

September 8, 2015

This week's *parashah* of Nitzavim ushers in and coincides with Rosh Hashanah and the Yamim Norayim, which is quite appropriate as the *parashah* contains the mitzvah regarding *teshuvah* – the entire theme of the High Holy Days: "...and you will return unto the Lord, your God, and hearken to His voice, according to all that I command you this day, you and your children, with all your heart and with all your soul, that then the Lord, your God, will turn your captivity and have compassion upon you."[22]

Chazal (the sages of the Talmud) also felt that there was a connection between the two based on the opening *pasuk*, which states, "You are standing today, all of you, before Hashem, your God..."

We too find ourselves every year standing before Hashem on the cusp of Rosh Hashanah (the New Year) and Yom Kippur (the Day of Atonement), and it is at this time that we must evaluate ourselves and our relationship with Hashem, whether we are indeed worthy to stand before Him, and if not, what we can do to improve our situation. This time of year is a time when each and every Jew should experience self-analysis and hopefully further his or her commitment to the Torah and its mitzvot.

There is no greater demonstration of subservience to Hashem than serving as a *chayal* in Tzahal, but it is still important to remember that for a Jewish *chayal*, this time of year demands introspection and more awareness toward the mitzvot. Try to further your rapport with Hashem and think about even small things that perhaps you can do to substantiate your allegiance to Him.

---

22   Deuteronomy 30:2–3.

Rosh Hashanah

September 13, 2015

Yakov,

The main mitzvah of Rosh Hashanah is hearing the shofar, the ram's horn which is also referred to in the Torah as a *keren*. What is the difference between calling it a shofar and a *keren*?

Rav Yakov Ariel explains that *keren* is from the Hebrew word *karnayim*, the horns of an animal, which provide it with its majesty and physical prowess. The brute force of a stag or a ram is based on the height and strength of its horns, and therefore the word *keren* refers to a material force. One can hold and touch the *keren*. The term *shofar* means something else; it is a derivative of the Hebrew word *shefoferet*, which means an air tube. One cannot touch or even describe the physical nature of air, and therefore the shofar refers to a spiritual entity.

On Rosh Hashanah one holds the *keren*, the physical horn, but what we are doing is blowing into the shofar, the air tube, and stating that we are interested in "seizing" the physical world and longing to be a part of a world that is higher and more significant; we aspire to convert physicality into something far more meaningful. It is for this reason that the *berachah* on the shofar is *"lishmoa kol shofar,"* to hear the sound of the shofar, as opposed to blowing the shofar (even though there is an opinion that the *berachah* should be "to blow the shofar"), because to blow is a physical act, but to hear or listen takes place in the abstract realm of the spiritual. On Rosh Hashanah we long to listen and to hear the shofar; we aspire to enter the realm of spirituality.

You are armed with *karnayim* in the form of physical weaponry and armament that provides you with brute strength; and at the same time, as someone who aspires to fulfill the mitzvot of Hashem, you understand the message of the shofar. May Hashem grant you the strength and understanding through your service to realize and succeed in both.

Shanah tovah (happy New Year).

▸ *Thank you, Abba. As far as I recall, the shofar was also used to call the Jewish people to arms, for example in the time of Yehoshua and the conquest of Eretz Canaan. When the shofar sounded, there was no differentiating between people. Anyone who heard the alarm of the shofar was expected to respond as part of the Jewish nation regardless of affiliation or level of observance. I think this is vital to remember particularly around Rosh Hashanah. Everyone is invited to hear the shofar and to respond in his or her particular fashion regardless of identity or depth of faith. The greatness of the institution of the army is its conduciveness to unity, and the beauty of Rosh Hashanah is its inclusiveness and the way it resonates with all of our people as a nation.*

Shana tovah to all.

Vayelech

September 21, 2015

Yakov,

Moshe informs Bnei Yisrael at the beginning of Parashat Vayelech (which we read this past Shabbat), "I am a hundred twenty years old today; I can no longer go out and come in..."[23]

Some explain that Moshe was saying he is incapable of "going out" and providing for the outer, materialistic needs of Bnei Yisrael and that he could not "come in," meaning he was incapable of offering an inner spiritual direction for them because he was out of touch with the people.

A great leader has to connect with his people, and he also needs the integrity to admit when he no longer can. You are now training to become a leader. To be effective, you have to commit to both the physical and spiritual welfare of our people. We are proud of you, and you should be proud as well. God willing your efforts will help facilitate a *gmar chatimah tovah* for all of the Jewish people.

---

23 Deuteronomy 31:2.

Haazinu

September 20, 2015

Yakov,

Parashat Haazinu is mostly a song which Moshe offers to Bnei Yisrael. In it, he relates the beauty of the Torah that he transmitted and requests, "May my teaching drop like the rain..."[24]

Rain is something that is not always easy to appreciate while it is falling because of its discomforts; its benefits are only recognizable after a period of time, after it has penetrated the depths of the earth, and fruit and produce begin to grow.

The same is true regarding the Torah and truthfully regarding most things that are intrinsically valuable and deeply insightful. Studying Torah can be taxing. It requires intense concentration and an intellectual investment that can be exhausting and even frustrating during the process. However, if one applies oneself and exhausts these efforts and energies toward Torah study, one will reap the huge benefits of what its wisdom has to offer. Often this wisdom is appreciated and finds application only years later, much like the produce from the rain, but it always proves to have been exceedingly worthwhile.

This principle is true regarding Eretz Yisrael as well. Eretz Yisrael is a challenging and difficult land, as is evident from the very fact that you are serving in the army; but all of our investments and even sacrifice for our homeland will prove worthwhile as we facilitate and ultimately experience the redemption of the Jewish people upon it.

Thank you for serving such an integral role in our redemption

Abba

---

24   Deuteronomy 32:2.

Yom Kippur

September 22, 2015

Yakov,

Yom Kippur is upon us.

We just read this past Shabbat from the *haftarah* of Shabbat Shuvah, in which the Navi Hosea beckons, "Return, Israel, to Hashem your God, for you have stumbled in your iniquity."[25]

If an accused is pending trial and judgment, and he realizes that he is not properly prepared to state his case, the one option he may have left is to seek audience directly with the overseer or judge and appeal on his own behalf, in the hope that the judge will sympathize with his predicament.

The problem with this option is that it is only available to certain select individuals who are granted access to the magistrate; most people are denied such an opportunity.

Am Yisrael, however, has a special rapport with Hashem; we are His children, as the *pasuk* confirms, "You are children to the Lord, your God…"[26]

We are considered Hashem's children, which is why we are granted access to Him every year to appeal and reestablish our loyalty to Him. Hashem, King of all kings, grants us the opportunity to return to Him, regardless of the fact that we "have stumbled in iniquity."

This is what Yom Kippur signifies: it is a day when we return to our Father in Heaven but also show appreciation for His offering us a private audience.

Mommy and I try to make ourselves accessible for you guys. Some of you take advantage of the opportunity to communicate more and

---

25   Hoshea 14:2.
26   Deuteronomy 14:1.

some less. When Hashem grants us this chance to speak openly with Him on this special day, we should maximize the opportunity.

Have a meaningful Yom Kippur, and *gmar chatimah tovah*.

Abba

▸ *Thanks a lot, Abba; it is a nice thought. Unfortunately, I am not sure how much time I will get for this audience with Hashem, because I won't have much time in shul; I have to do guard duty. If I cannot be in shul for large parts of the* tefillah, *what do you recommend I say with the time that I have?*

First, I would deal with the regular obligations of *tefillah*, and I would try to say the Amidah prayer for each *tefillah*. Reciting the Amidah will also ensure that you recite Viduy (confession), which according to the Rambam is the mitzvah of *teshuvah*. I would also say *berachot* and Shema, and then anything else you can add on after that is a bonus.

Regarding your short audience with Hashem, I remember once reading somewhere (I don't remember where) how ridiculous it is when people scream their *tefillot* out in shul as if Hashem is hard of hearing. He can hear them just as well when they whisper. Similarly, Hashem is not bound to time, because He is Infinite, and so whatever time you can allocate to daven to Him is valuable beyond our comprehension. From wherever you are, whatever time you have on Yom Kippur to concentrate and daven to Hashem, even if just a few moments, will I am sure be worthwhile, particularly considering the circumstances and mitzvot that you are involved in as a *chayal*.

▸ *That makes sense. I want to thank you for being a wonderful parent and for offering me your support, not only in the army, but through everything. I know it is typically hard for me to express myself, and I am not* very talkative, but I really do appreciate what you and Mommy do. If I slighted you in any way, I ask for mechilah. Hashem should grant you a great year and a lot of strength to continue doing your great work for Am Yisrael. Gmar chatimah tovah *and love you*.

What is the Viduy you say every year on Yom Kippur?

I think you are referring to the fact that every year I try to say the Viduy of the Chayei Adam, who spells out specific sins that fall out alphabetically under the main categories of the Viduy. It is quite extensive, and I am not sure you will have time to delineate and say the whole thing. If you do find time, it is quite significant to say or even just to read through it as a way of familiarizing yourself with various sins that people commit and enhancing your concentration while saying the Viduy.

▶ *Thanks. Just two more days and Yom Kippur will be over and you can fly home.* Gmar chatimah tovah.

In two days it is not "over," rather everything is just beginning. We should have a *shanah tovah*.

Sukkot

September 30, 2015

The sukkah reminds us that our physical existence is temporary, while our spiritual values are eternal, hence we leave the comforts of our permanent home and dwell in a temporary, less comfortable dwelling for seven days. In addition, the sukkah unifies us as we congregate within the confines of its walls, exemplifying how the Jewish people were surrounded as a nation by the Clouds of Glory in the desert.

During the holiday of Sukkot, upon the conclusion of a Shemittah year,[27] we are expected to perform the mitzvah of *hak'hel* (from the word *kahal* [congregation]); all of Bnei Yisrael gather in Yerushalayim to hear words of the Torah read as one: "Assemble the people, the men and the women and the little ones…that they may hear, and that they may learn, and fear the Lord your God, and observe to do all the words of this law."[28]

The Gemara explains that the reason small children were brought to participate in this mitzvah, even though they are not obligated in the mitzvot, is "to give reward to those who bring them,"[29] but I believe there is another significant reason. While children might not be obligated in mitzvot, they are highly impressionable. When they witness a large gathering, they learn to appreciate not only the event itself, but also what it means to be part of a collective known as a nation.

In a similar vein, every year we stand during the reading of the Ten Commandments, reenacting Bnei Yisrael's acceptance of the Torah at

---

27   Shemittah is the Sabbatical year during which the land lies fallow in fulfillment of the biblical requirement to rest the land every seventh year per Exodus 23:10–11 and Leviticus 25:1–7.
28   Deuteronomy 31:12.
29   Babylonian Talmud, *Chagigah* 3a.

Sinai. Although the event at Sinai took place long ago, the importance of feeling part of a *kahal* must remain eternal.

You may not be home for Sukkot, but remember that you not only merit belonging to a nation, but that you are responsible for securing its future.

Chag sameach.

October 1, 2015

The Midrash, *Leviticus Rabbah* compares all four species to four different types of Jews. Those Jews who adhere both to the mitzvot and Torah study are compared to the *etrog* (citrus), which has both taste and a pleasing scent. On the other hand, the *aravah* (willow) is a plant that has neither a scent nor a taste, and therefore the Midrash compares it to Jews who are void of Torah knowledge and do not perform mitzvot. Nonetheless, bringing all four species together demonstrates the strength of unity and that each Jew is responsible for the next, regardless of their level of observance.

On the last day of Sukkot, Hoshanah Rabbah, only the willow is left upright on the side of the Altar in the Mikdash, symbolizing that even the weakest of individuals can learn to stand independently, if taught and encouraged in a positive environment. The successful education of a child or student is measured by the ability to provide him with the strength and resilience to believe in himself, regardless of the challenges that lie ahead.

You should be proud of how you have overcome adversity. Although there are many challenges yet to come, we are confident that by unifying with those around you and sharing a common purpose, you will all know success.

Chag sameach.

Vezot Haberachah

October 2, 2015

Vezot Haberachah, the last *parashah* in the Torah, describes Bnei Yisrael's mourning the demise of Moshe: "then the days of tearful mourning for Moshe ended."[30]

The Torah also describes the conclusion of the mourning period for our forefather Yakov: "When his bewailing period passed..."[31] Why is the mourning period for Yakov described as having "passed," whereas regarding Moshe the Torah concludes that the mourning "ended"?

The Midrash comments that no one cried when Moshe died, and so his mourning period "ended," but Yakov's passing caused people to cry, and therefore his mourning "passed" but never really ended.[32] This too is difficult to understand.

In his commentary *Oznayim La'Torah*, Rabbi Sorotzkin explains the midrash as saying that following the death of Yakov and the mourning of his passing, Bnei Yisrael knew that they would have to stay in Egypt for a long period of time, and so the bitterness of the mourning "passed" but it did not "end"; Bnei Yisrael continued to cry, as they remained strangers in a strange land. Yet with the passing of Moshe, Bnei Yisrael would enter Eretz Yisrael, which was an essential goal; therefore they did not cry, and their mourning for Moshe "ended."

As a *chayal*, you become an integral part of securing the goal of living in Eretz Yisrael, and regardless of the challenges and obstructions you will inevitably experience, being able to do so is a great source of comfort.

Abba

---

30   Deuteronomy 34:8.
31   Genesis 50:4.
32   Midrash, *Genesis Rabbah* 100:4.

Advanced Basic Training: Genesis

Following basic training, combat soldiers go through at least another three and half months of advanced basic training. While during this time strict discipline is still enforced, the emphasis is less on discipline and more on actually using advanced weaponry and applying combat skills. Soldiers are assigned specific jobs within their divisions and camaraderie within the division is solidified.

Bereishit

Rashi explains that the Torah begins with the words "In the beginning of God's creating the heavens and the earth…," based on the Midrash which quotes Rav Yitzchak as saying that the Torah should have begun with the first commandment of sanctifying the new moon, the first law that was addressed to all of Jewry as a nation. However the Torah began with the narrative of Creation to establish that Hashem is Sovereign of the universe, and should the nations accuse Am Yisrael of thievery for conquering the Eretz Yisrael from the seven Canaanite nations, they can respond that the entire universe belongs to Hashem, and He can desire to give it to whomever He sees fit.

Although this midrash is rather challenging to understand, it is important to appreciate that it demonstrates that the creation of the world is premised upon the ability for Am Yisrael to possess Eretz Yisrael. From the very outset of Creation, one of the reasons for the existence of the universe has been to grant the Jewish people the Land of Israel, which you merit to preserve and protect. That must be comforting particularly as you too begin a new chapter in your service with your advanced basic training.

Noach

October 15, 2015

As you are well aware, our mitzvot fall into one of two categories: the first is referred to as *bein adam la'Makom* (between man and Hashem) and the second is *bein adam l'chavero* (between man and his fellow). Both constitute a means by which to demonstrate our subservience to Hashem.

Prior to the flood that would destroy the world, the Torah says, "And the earth was corrupt before God; and the earth was filled with robbery."[33]

The verse indicates a breakdown in the two institutions that preserve the world: "the earth was corrupt before God" signifies failure by man to connect with Hashem, and "the earth was filled with robbery" suggests a collapse in man's ability to relate to his fellow man.

When we understand what caused the destruction of the world, we can then appreciate that the only way to rebuild it and assure its permanence is by establishing a rapport with Hashem and heightening sensitivity toward the people around us. When you guard over our land and nation, you fulfill *bein adam la'Makom*, and in protecting our citizens and uniting with your fellow soldiers, you fulfill *bein adam l'chavero*.

Serving in Tzahal gives you a chance to exemplify a wholesome Jew, and in that merit, you should know success during this difficult time of your training.

▶ *Thank you for your inspirational words, Abba. Unfortunately, the two institutions that I know are crucial often conflict with each other. For example, as a religious soldier, I have extra time in the morning to*

---

33   Genesis 6:11.

daven Shacharit, but while I do so, the secular soldiers in our division have to prepare the equipment for the day's maneuvers and training, which takes them longer because we (observant soldiers) are not there to help. They do not say anything, but I have a strong feeling this does not sit well with our secular comrades. These are some of the challenges we knew we would have to deal with as religious soldiers in a mixed unit, challenges that a beinish [bnei yeshivot] Hesder yeshiva unit does not have because they serve as a unit of religious observant soldiers together, and therefore they do not have to deal with these sensitive situations as much as we do.

I remain committed to my davening and to serving Hashem as best I can, but I must put in extra effort during the course of the day to demonstrate to my fellow soldiers my concern for them and for the duty at hand.

The mechinah prepared us for these circumstances and taught us to sensitize ourselves to these types of scenarios so as not to cause a chillul Hashem (desecration of God's Name). Learning about it in theory is much easier than confronting it in practice.

I understand your difficulty. It is interesting to note that although there was an obvious breakdown in both primary institutions mentioned above, the Torah emphasizes that Hashem destroyed the world by means of the flood because "…all flesh corrupted its way upon the earth."[34] The world was filled with what the Torah calls *hamas*, which Rashi explains is thievery and plundering.

The Torah does not say anywhere explicitly that the world was destroyed because of a lack of belief in Hashem or even because of the

---

34 Genesis 6:12.

idolatry they practiced. The destruction was the result of the disregard toward another person's property, a lack of *bein adam l'chavero* – man's conduct toward and respect for his fellow man.

This is a pattern that repeats itself consistently throughout the Torah. Many people are enthralled by God and spirituality, but they give themselves a pass on the basics of *derech eretz* (proper behavior toward others); they are inconsiderate and insensitive toward their fellow. The Torah says that if one wants to get through to Hashem, he first has to learn how to deal with his fellow man, which is usually more challenging.

This is why almost all the mitzvot given to Bnei Yisrael following their receiving of the Torah at Sinai have to do with *bein adam l'chavero*. It is also for this reason that prior to Yom Kippur, one must ask forgiveness from the people around him, and if one does not, indeed he is not forgiven for any of the transgressions he may have committed, including those that are *bein adam la'Makom*.

There is no institution today in the Jewish world that demonstrates dedication and devotion to *bein adam l'chavero* more than Tzahal. I believe this is a fundamental that your fellow *chayalim* admire and respect about you. Your service in Tzahal and that of your comrades therefore represent the means of rebuilding a world that will help you get closer to understanding God.

▶ *Thanks. Sorry I could not speak to you for too long before; we are so limited with the amount of time we have on our phones. Look forward to seeing you all next Shabbat.*

Shavua Milchamah – War Week

This particular week during intensive basic training is a very difficult one that all combat soldiers have to endure. It is the first time that soldiers spend an entire week as they would if God forbid they had to go out to war. The food they receive during this week is battle rations, and of course they have no access to their phones the entire week. I felt the following dvar Torah *was appropriate to the challenging situation that Yakov was about to confront.*

October 16, 2015

The Torah says at the beginning of Parashat Noach that "God walked Noah."[35]

The Netziv explains in his commentary *Ha'amek Davar* that Noah was not concerned enough about his generation. He did not reprimand their behavior, and for that reason, he was not righteous enough to stand on his own; he had to rely on God to "walk" him and steer him in the right direction, which demonstrates a certain weakness.

Similarly, the Talmud says: "Abaye said, 'Those rabbinic leaders whose constituents love them, it is not necessarily because of their greatness, but because they don't reprimand their constituents toward greater spiritual behavior [and the people are happy that their rabbinic leaders leave them alone]."[36]

A leader who does not reprimand his followers is clearly not doing his job; which is why, if a leader is loved by everyone, chances are it is because he leaves them alone to do as they please.

---

35 Genesis 6:9.
36 Babylonian Talmud, *Ketubot* 105b.

I don't enjoy reprimanding you, knowing what you go through in the army; it is uncomfortable for me to do so during the short time you come home. However, if I do not reprimand or guide you, then I too am not fulfilling my job as a parent, as Shlomo Hamelech wrote, "One who spares his rod hates his child, but he who loves him disciplines him in his youth."[37]

In the army it is only natural to experience spiritual downfalls, because it is challenging to maintain a strong spiritual level when you are immersed in physical training and bound to someone else's scheduling and dictating policy. Therefore, it is vital that you not compromise on certain spiritual basics, such as putting on tefillin, wearing tzitzit, refraining from talking during *tefillot* and Kaddish, and trying to find even a few minutes every day to learn some Torah. Try to ensure that these basics remain first and foremost as part of your commitments, regardless of the challenging circumstances you find yourself in.

The reason I send you the daily *divrei Torah* is to provide you with easy access to learning something every day. This is also why they print so many of these little booklets and pamphlets that you find in the army, because they know it is difficult for the average *chayal* to open a *sefer* and immerse himself in learning. These abridged pamphlets make learning readily accessible.

You are beginning a new process in the army. It is very important not only to remember who you are, but also to assert who you are, based on incorporating your daily spiritual obligations into your routine army ones.

We are proud of you, and we are confident that you can stay strong and maintain an existence by which you are "walking with God" as well.

---

37 Proverbs 13:24.

Lech Lecha

October 18, 2015

I know that you are spending the week in intensive training out in the field, and it is probably very challenging, so here are a few words of encouragement.

Hashem instructs Avram at the beginning of Parashat Lech Lecha, "Go for yourself from your land…"[38]

Rashi comments, "For your own benefit and for your own good." Many commentaries explain that Hashem's directive was a test of Avram's loyalty, but if Avram was leaving his land for his own benefit as Rashi explained, how would this prove his devotion to Hashem?

Immediately following Hashem's directive to Avram, the Torah confirms: "So, Abram went, as the Lord had spoken to him…"[39]

Avram left his birthplace "as the Lord had spoken to him"; there were no personal incentives or calculations, rather a firm commitment to fulfill Hashem's instruction.

When performing a mitzvah, we should ask ourselves what our motivations are. Are we fulfilling the mitzvah for personal gain, or are we doing so out of devotion to Hashem?

Like Avram, you too were challenged to leave your family and home, but you are doing so in order to protect our land and to preserve our nation – the same nation and land that was promised to Avram so long ago. Serving in Tzahal is an outstanding mitzvah that you perform untainted by personal interest and in the hope of fulfilling a dream "as the Lord had spoken to him."

---

38   Genesis 12:1.
39   Genesis 12:4.

44 | *Armed with Spirit*

▶ *I think another difference is that Avram was on his own; it is obviously not as challenging for me because I am with a* chevrah. *We are all in the same boat, and whether my comrades see it altruistically or not, we are all fulfilling the same service. Although many of the guys are not observant and are uneducated with regard to the Torah, I think most of them have some appreciation of how historically significant our biblical land is to the Jewish people.*

You and I know that many religious guys choose to learn in Hesder yeshivot and opt to serve in Hesder beinish *units. We are well aware of what they consider the advantage they have regarding serving with religious people like themselves, interacting less with the secular soldiers in the army and protecting themselves from endangering their level of religious commitment. Many of them may even see their shorter service as an advantage as well. I opted to serve the full thirty-two months in the army because I felt that it was only fair and correct to serve the same amount of time as all soldiers have to (particularly those secular soldiers who don't have the option of shortening the active part of their service as the* beinishim *do).*[40]

Yet I realize with time that I am at an advantage as well because I have the opportunity to socialize and interact with my secular companions. This gives me exposure to all walks of society in Eretz Yisrael, and I can come to terms with my secular peers' experiences and

---

40   Hesder units in the army serve a longer term overall (five years as opposed to thirty-two months), but a shorter portion of it (sixteen months) is spent in active duty, the remainder being spent in Torah learning.

feelings as well. I can begin to understand where they and their attitudes toward observant people in Israel come from, and this is important if not for the sake of problem solving, at least for the sake of understanding. Additionally, so many secular Israelis have never been exposed to observant people, and their perception of them can be skewed. Tzahal provides us with an opportunity to live side by side, to learn from one another, and consequently to respect and even admire each other's views.

This is all true, and we have discussed this in the past. While I am confident in your upholding your observance, I believe it is important to remind you that given this opportunity to discuss and compare with your nonobservant friends and to share with them your ideals from a religious perspective, your commitment becomes even more crucial as a result of the scrutiny you invite upon yourself.

Vayera

October 27, 2015

The Midrash says that one of the things we learn from Avraham's desire to invite weary travelers and guests into his home is that "greeting people and providing for them is a greater mitzvah than going to greet the Divine Presence of Hashem."[41] How is this conceivable?

The Avnei Nezer has a unique way of explaining this equation: Avraham could have spent more time nurturing his own relationship with Hashem; had he done so, he would have reached even greater spiritual heights, enjoying even closer rapport with Hashem. Yet he chose to expend his resources to bring more people closer to monotheism and away from idolatry. This is what is meant in the midrash: "greeting people and providing for them" was more significant to Avraham "than going to greet the Divine Presence of Hashem."

At times a person must sacrifice his personal concerns and growth for the sake of serving the public and facilitating the spiritual growth of a nation, precisely what you are fulfilling through your service in the army. All *chayalim* regardless of adherence or nonadherence to halachah connect to Avraham our forefather in this way."

A few days ago you wrote to me regarding the advantage that *beinishim* have serving in Tzahal as a religious unit, but even *beinishim* are aware of the challenges of preserving intensive religiosity and strict observance in the framework of the army. You cannot possibly learn Torah with the same efficiency when you are in the army as you did in the *mechinah*, and you cannot daven with the same intensity when you are in the army, where one is not granted the same time for spiritual growth as you were when you studied in the *mechinah*. But you all are occupied "greeting people and providing for them."

---

41   Midrash, *Psalms Rabbah* 18.

▶ *Abba, I think it is so important for people to realize that when we talk about the "sacrifice" which we make as chayalim, that translates in many ways. The most obvious sacrifice is that of one's life, God forbid, but sacrifice in a less extreme way such as giving one's time or having to prioritize differently is also a form of giving. When someone who is dedicated to learning Torah and loves sitting and learning joins the army, he undoubtedly sacrifices because he may no longer be capable of maintaining his intense study. Similarly, every* chayal, *observant and nonobservant alike, sacrifices the ability to pursue academia or further a career during the time of service. I am not looking for credit, and quite frankly I don't think most* chayalim *are, but at the end of the day, something has got to give, and what you are proposing in the name of the Avnei Nezer is comforting. When you think about what he has suggested, I am not sure how those who don't serve in the army are comfortable with themselves.*

Chayei Sarah

November 1, 2015

"Abraham came to eulogize Sarah and to bewail her."[42] The Midrash comments, "Where did Abraham come from? He came from Mount Moriah." What does the Midrash reveal by telling us that Avraham came from Mount Moriah, something which is rather obvious?

Perhaps the Midrash is offering a message with regard to Sarah's greatness and Avraham's desire to reveal her prominence. The Midrash is not inquiring about Avraham's physical location, but rather about his spiritual voyage: How did Avraham reach his spiritual heights and acquire his outstanding attributes? Avraham, who came to eulogize and mourn Sarah, wanted to reveal that his strength and greatness came from her. Therefore the Midrash answers that Avraham came from Mount Moriah, the place where Yitzchak was willing to offer himself for sacrifice. Only a child with an outstanding mother such as Sarah would even consider doing such a thing. The Midrash confirms that Avraham's ability to infuse a willingness in Yitzchak to offer himself at Mount Moriah was ultimately the result of the outstanding character and strength of Sarah.

▶ *Abba! Here is a thought that Rav Eli sent to us from the* mechinah, *which I wanted to share with you on a similar note.*

Rashi suggests that the immediate cause of Sarah's demise was the shock she experienced when she heard that her beloved son, Yitzchak, was being offered as a sacrifice. Rashi uses the words "her soul fled" from her body, presumably as a result of the alarming news. Yet

---

42 Genesis 23:2.

there is an additional meaning to how Rashi describes Sarah's reaction, and that is "her soul flourished" from her body. Sarah was revived, and her last breath was exhilarated with the knowledge that she succeeded in raising a son who was willing to give up his life in service of Hashem.

Thanks for sharing. Apropos of what you texted yesterday when you mentioned how important it was for people to recognize the preparedness of *chayalim* to sacrifice: although it is difficult for us to comprehend that a mother would be exhilarated to know that her son was prepared to give his life for Hashem, this too represents the sacrifice that every parent of a *chayal* makes. We will miss you on Shabbat, but as parents we are comforted to know that we too have a son who is willing to sacrifice in service of Hashem and the Jewish people.

► *That is really not such a fair comparison, but I appreciate your praise and words of encouragement.*
   Shabbat shalom.

Toldot

November 9, 2015

Yakov,

I am sure you are familiar with the midrash on the *pasuk* "The children [Yakov and Esav] struggled together within her [Rivkah's womb],"[43] to which the Midrash comments, "When Rivkah passed the Torah academy of Shem and Ever, Yakov struggled to come forth, and when she passed a temple of idol worship, Esav struggled to come forth."[44]

The Talmud says that when a baby is in its mother's womb, an angel sits and studies Torah with the fetus the entire time. Rabbi Chaim Shmuelevitz asks, if this is the case, why did Yakov struggle to leave his mother's womb when he could have stayed in the womb studying Torah?

Rabbi Shmuelevitz explains that even as a babe Yakov understood that things are more valuable when they are earned through hard work and diligence. Yakov longed to leave his mother's womb and enter the physical world, where the challenges to grow spiritually would be an increasingly significant accomplishment. Last week I mentioned to you that Rivkah's drawing water out of the well represented her understanding that without work and effort, one cannot truly benefit from this world; it appears that this consideration was transmitted to Rivkah's son Yakov as well.

This premise is voiced by Chazal in Mishnah *Avot*: "According to the pain [effort] is the reward."[45]

Serving in the army is difficult, as you know well. Not only because of the physical training and mental disciplines involved regarding any

---

43 Genesis 25:22.
44 Midrash, *Genesis Rabbah* 63:6.
45 *Avot* 5:23.

army, but particularly because you are serving in the Israeli army, as the Talmud says, "Eretz Yisrael is acquired through our struggles."[46]

It is crucial to remember that according to the efforts you invest is the amount of reward and benefits you will secure.

▶ *Abba, I imagine that part of the reason the pain is so rewarding is that when you are in the middle of a struggle, it is difficult to appreciate what you are doing it for. When you are immersed in the day to day of the army, you get wrapped up in things and don't really see the big picture; every run, exercise, and training drill is tedious, but ultimately for the furtherance of Am Yisrael and to secure Eretz Yisrael. I will try to remember this message and internalize it.*

The challenge of being immersed in the day to day and forgetting to see the big picture is something we confront in everything we do in life, including going to work, raising a family, or the many functions that become routine but that we are really supposed to appreciate. I think this is part of the idea of establishing *berachot* particularly on different functions and things we enjoy. Prior to engaging, seeing, tasting, or hearing, we pause a moment and reflect upon the opportunity presented to us, which at first glance might seem mundane but is an opportunity nonetheless. Making a *berachah* encourages us not only to elevate the ordinary but to appreciate everyday functions and routines by designating purpose to them through the recital of a *berachah*. If this is the case regarding the "usual" routines we go through, how much more so does it apply to the opportunities you mentioned.

---

46   Babylonian Talmud, *Berachot* 5a.

Vayetzei

November 15, 2015

The Torah informs us where Yakov was leaving from and where he was headed to: "Yakov departed from Beer Sheva and went toward Haran."[47]

The Beis Halevi explains that generally speaking, when a person is traveling somewhere, he is not concerned about his point of departure as much as his destination. Yakov however demonstrated meaning in both. He fulfilled the mitzvah of respecting Rivkah, his mother, both by leaving Beer Sheva as she had instructed him ("Now therefore, my son, hearken to my voice, and arise; flee…to Haran"[48]) and by going to Haran because Rivkah wanted Yakov to marry a girl from Haran and not from Canaan.

People of significance and virtue always look for ways to inspire. Wherever they are coming from and whichever direction they are moving in, they seek positive influence.

The words describing your forefather with whom you share the same name, "Yakov departed…and went toward," become that much more meaningful.

---

47   Genesis 28:10.
48   Genesis 27:43.

Vayishlach

November 24, 2015

Yakov,

I hope you are enjoying your few days off; they are well deserved, and I am sorry I could not be there with you.

The Torah says that Yakov sent "messengers ahead of him to Esav his brother, to the land of Seir."[49] One opinion in Rashi says that Yakov sent real angels ahead of him. If the reason Yakov sent angels ahead of him was to plan militarily for his confrontation with his brother Esav, why was it necessary for him to send real angels as opposed to sending scouts?

The Mishnah in *Avot* says, "Distance yourself from a bad neighbor, and do not associate with wickedness."[50] The Mishnah suggests that we avoid two entities, both a bad neighbor and wickedness in general. Yakov understood this, and he was wary of the people he was around as well as the place where he resided; hence he sent real angels to ensure protection both from the influence of Esav and from the wickedness of the land of Edom. The angels and protectors to which Rashi refers represent the Torah observances that Yakov used to protect himself from the threatening influences around him.

One of our jobs in life is to identify problems before we confront them; we have to know whom we should avoid and how to stay away from trouble. I am sure that many times you are exhausted, and it is more convenient to daven quickly, or without a minyan, or even to skip a *tefillah*. I am sure at times the unit is together and the guys are conversing improperly, and it is easier to join in. All of these situations are tempting, and you may have to "send angels ahead" for your spiritual

---

49   Genesis 32:4.
50   *Pirkei Avot* 1:7.

preservation. At times you have to protect yourself from various influences and look for ways to influence those around you.

► *No question about it, Abba. We are restricted in the time we have to daven, and there is some peer pressure. In the* mechinah *they often spoke about being different because of religion. They also warned us not to use religion as an excuse to be different. For example, they said that, even though as religious guys we can get a* ptor zakan *(permission to grow a beard for religious reasons), we should not use it but rather should take the extra time to shave every day like everyone else. If we demonstrate too many differences because of religion, particularly if they are seen as privileges because of our observance, it can lead to resentment toward us and toward Judaism in general.*

I appreciate your insight and advice and will try to be careful not to compromise my observance as well.

Vayeshev

December 1, 2015

When Yosef went out to the fields looking for his brothers, according to his father's instructions, he came across a man who asked him, "What do you seek?"[51] to which Yosef answered, "My brothers I do seek."[52]

Although this is not the simple understanding, perhaps the Torah wants a Jew to always be in the mode of "My brothers I do seek"; his prayers and service should demonstrate that he is primarily concerned with his brothers as opposed to himself.

In today's Jewish world there is no greater example of those who "seek the welfare of their brothers" than *chayalim* who serve in Tzahal.

---

51 Genesis 37:16.
52 Genesis 37:17.

Miketz: Chanukah on Base

December 11, 2017

Yakov,

Parashat Miketz always falls out on Shabbat Chanukah. One suggestion offered for the connection of Miketz to Chanukah is that in Miketz, Pharaoh dreams about seven skinny weak cows swallowing seven fat stronger cows and seven slight sheaves of wheat devouring seven hefty ones; both dreams were outstanding signs of Yosef's success. Similarly, on Chanukah a dream occurred. The small and seemingly weak Jewish army of the Maccabim devoured and defeated the mighty army of the Greek empire, which was obviously beneficial for Am Yisrael. Both Pharaoh's dreams and the story of Chanukah establish that the strength of Am Yisrael does not originate from wealth, stature, or physical might; rather it comes from the spirit.

"Not by military force, and not by power, but by My spirit, says the lord of hosts."[53]

Happy Chanukah!

▶ *That is a really nice thought, Abba. I think it is important to note though that the miracle of Yosef's salvation from his incarceration in Egypt only happened after Yosef used his initiative to interpret the dreams of the butler and baker while he was in jail, which afforded him the opportunity to interpret Pharaoh's dream as well. The miracle of the defeat of the Greek armies by the Maccabim also only transpired after the Maccabim took arms against the Greeks and declared that they would*

---

53   Zechariah 4:6.

no longer stand for their persecution. In other words, as a religious person I try to understand the value of believing in Hashem and the strength we receive from this belief. As a religious chayal I also appreciate that without our investment in an institution and our involvement in a cause, the spiritual components from Hashem do not necessarily reveal themselves blatantly. Hashem expects from us to activate and participate, and when we do, He then reveals His presence in the form of salvation.

I agree with what you are saying a hundred percent, as do Chazal in many places. One of the most obvious places we see what you are proposing revealed is where we find ourselves right now, Chanukah.

We celebrate Chanukah because of the miracle of the small flask of oil, which had enough oil to last one day but remained lit for eight days. One of the famous questions regarding Chanukah is why we celebrate eight days if there was enough oil for one day: one of the days was not miraculous at all, so shouldn't we celebrate only seven days of Chanukah?

I believe there are over one hundred answers that address this question; one is from Rabbi Yosef Karo in the *Beit Yosef*. He explains that Hashem rarely generates miracles from nothingness; rather He uses existing matter. Therefore, the bit of oil in the flask had to initiate the miracle in order to remain lit for the next seven days, and since the first day was an integral part of the miracle, we celebrate eight days of Chanukah and not seven. This concept applies to us and our approach to Eretz Yisrael today as well. Eretz Yisrael demands our involvement and that we initiate activity in order to uncover the Land's potential both physically and spiritually. Once we invest in development of the land, Hashem will facilitate a successful and miraculous future in Israel. The greatest demonstration of this are *chayalei Tzahal*, who show that they want to participate in the future of Eretz Yisrael. Through your efforts may we be privileged to see Hashem's Hand in our redemption and again partake from the light of the Menorah in the Beit Hamikdash.

Happy Chanukah.

Kav – in the Line of Duty, Hevron: Genesis/Exodus/Leviticus/Numbers

Kav in Hebrew literally means line. This is the time combat soldiers have been training for, as they are dispersed and divided according to their divisions to guard the various borders around Israel. The Kfir Brigade generally guards Judea and Samaria. The other major combat brigades, Tzanchanim, Givati, Golani, and Nahal, all spend time on various borders and guarding positions including the Gaza border, Egyptian and Syrian borders, and the main hotbed of terrorist attacks, Hevron. This marked an intense time of Yakov's service, and I felt that spiritual sustenance was particularly vital.

Vayigash

December 18, 2015

I saw a beautiful insight which I wanted to share with you. The Torah describes the gifts that Yosef sent his father, Yakov, from Egypt as follows: "ten he-donkeys laden with the best of Egypt."[54]

Rashi explains based on the Talmud that "the best of Egypt" refers to "old wine, which eases the mind of old people." What does this mean?

The Mishnah in *Avot* says, "Rabbi Meir says, 'Do not look at the jug but at what is in it; there can be a new jug filled with old wine, and an old one without even new wine in it.'"[55]

Yosef knew that the moment his father heard that he was viceroy of Egypt, Yakov would worry that as an Egyptian, Yosef's main priorities would be aesthetics and outer appearance. This is precisely why Yosef sent to Yakov old wine, to demonstrate to Yakov that he had not become concerned with externals, but rather still recognized the meaning of inner characteristics, like the wine inside the barrel.

Be strong, never fear outer appearances, and march to the beat of your inner spirit.

Shabbat shalom.

▶ *Thank you. You know this is really the first time I have been exposed to secular Israelis and their way of thinking. I am amazed at how little they know about the foundations and basics of our tradition and how uninterested some of them are. Some say they see no difference between Eretz Yisrael and all other countries; they do*

---

54 Genesis 45:23.
55 *Pirkei Avot* 4:20.

not feel a "Jewish" connection or appreciate calling Israel
the "Jewish Homeland," to the extent that they would
have no problem living in a different country. Although
I have heard about this phenomenon before, it is differ-
ent when you see it and live with it on a daily basis. I
feel blessed to have grown up in a home based in tradi-
tion, which encourages us to understand the advantages
of living here.

I am glad to hear how you feel. As I said above, you are frustrated for the right reasons. I often tell people that I ask secular soldiers which is the only Jewish institution in the world that unites people, and they always answer that it is the shul. I then retort that this is a sign that they have never been to a shul, because if they had they would know that unfortunately the shul today is divisive. The only institution in the Jewish world today that unifies is Tzahal; the army presents you with an opportunity to show that the Jewish people are capable of uniting. Rabbi Lau always says that the Holocaust taught the Jewish people how to die together, and the Land of Israel should teach the Jewish people how to live together.

Parashat Vayechi, which is upcoming, describes how Yakov approached the end of his life. He gathered his sons together to give them *berachot*, as it says, "Gather yourselves together, that I may tell you what will befall you in the end of days [the time of the arrival of the Messiah]."[56]

One commentary explains that, although in the end Yakov could not reveal to his sons what would happen in the end of days, he did manage to transmit a vital message to his children on how to facilitate the arrival of the Messiah. The first thing Yakov told his sons was to "gather together," because unity is the only way to ensure redemption. The Hebrew word used by Yakov to transmit the message was *v'aggidah* (I

---

56   Genesis 49:1.

will tell you). *V'aggidah* also comes from the Hebrew root *egged*, which literally means unite. Yakov *told* his sons that the redemption of the Jewish people can only transpire by gathering together and uniting.

I would not engage head on in your frustrations; demonstrate through example and look at the army as a means of uniting the Jewish people. Don't grow irritated with your secular peers; rather find the themes and causes that all of you share in common because of and during your service.

▶ *Easier said than done, but I couldn't agree more.*

No one said anything would be easy; usually the things that are extremely valuable and worthwhile are also the most challenging.

Vayechi

December 25, 2015

Yakov,

Here is an important message not only for your time serving in the army but for life in general.

In the *haftarah* of Parashat Vayechi, David Hamelech calls his son Shlomo to offer him a *berachah* prior to his departure from this world, much as Yakov did with his sons in Parashat Vayechi; hence the connection between the *parashah* and the *haftarah*. David opens by saying to Shlomo, "I go the way of all the earth; be strong therefore, and become a man,"[57] a truly remarkable statement.

The first thing that the great David Hamelech chooses to say to Shlomo is that he is human like anyone else. David reveals humility and a deep sense of reality. In addition, the first piece of advice and guidance that he offers Shlomo is "be strong therefore, and become a man." One would think that David has greater aspirations for his son and would encourage him to become a righteous scholar. Yet David's message rings loud and clear: prior to becoming a righteous or pious individual, one must first "become a man." A person needs to acquire the common sense and understanding with which to become a decent human being. This is what we refer to as *"derech eretz kadmah"* (human decency prior to anything else).

---

57   I Kings 2:2.

Shemot

December 27, 2015

This week we begin the book of Exodus, which opens, "And these are the names of the Children of Israel who are coming to Egypt."[58]

Many of the commentaries ask why the Torah refers to the Children of Israel "who are coming to Egypt," in the present tense, when in actuality the Children of Israel had already come down to Egypt?

The Chidushei Harim, the Rebbe of Gur, explains that throughout Jewish history, with all of our challenges and difficulties, the names of the Children of Israel are consistently "coming" to preserve our identity and to ensure that our affiliation remains intact. We reflect upon who we are, but we are always interested in "coming" and moving forward; this is what provides us with resilience to survive even in places like Egypt.

Yakov, a *chayal* was stabbed this morning in Yerushalayim; Baruch Hashem he is okay, but please be alert and look after yourself. May Hashem grant you the strength to fulfill your important mission. I love you.

▶ *Will do, don't worry. Baruch Hashem the* chayal *is okay.*

I am reviewing the portion of Gemara that we learned together while you were home; thank you for taking the time to learn with me.

▶ *You're funny, Abba, no problem at all.*

---

58 Exodus 1:1.

January 1, 2016

When Hashem appeared to Moshe for the first time, He instructed, "Do not come closer to here; take off your shoes from your feet, for the place upon which you stand is holy ground."[59]

The Malbim explains that a person who wants to be a spiritual leader of significance must find the deeper meaning of his mission, as well as the intrinsic value of those whom he leads – precisely what Hashem expected from Moshe. When Hashem instructed Moshe to remove his shoes, He was teaching him to remove himself from the physical entities of the world and concern himself with what comes from within, such as belief and sanctity; only then can a person appreciate the meaning of the world.

Right now, you are sitting out in the rain and cold, and it is probably difficult for you to see beyond the discomfort you are experiencing, but at such times remember to "take off your shoes."

▸ *I just read yesterday's and today's* divrei Torah *because I did not have time until now, and I appreciate the words of encouragement.*
   Go Bengals!

---

59   Exodus 3:5.

Vaera

January 25, 2017

I saw a beautiful insight from Rabbi Meir Shapiro, the founder of the Daf Hayomi. Hashem told Moshe, "Take your rod, and cast it down before Pharaoh, that it will become a serpent."[60] The casting of the staff in front of Pharaoh represents Bnei Yisrael's being cast into Egyptian society, where they were badly influenced and began to subscribe to the Egyptian gods. Rav Shapiro explains that people are subject to their environment and the wrong atmosphere can be corruptive. However, the reverse is true as well. The Torah attests that once the rod or staff turned into a snake it could turn back into a staff again: "The Lord said to Moses, 'Put forth your hand, and take it [the snake] by the tail' – and he put forth his hand, and laid hold of it, and it became a rod in his hand."[61]

This shows that the moment a person finds himself in the right surroundings, it becomes conducive for him to change and improve.

I would add that the staff represented Moshe's "security blanket" as well, and the concept that Rav Shapiro is sharing with us is that good leaders surround themselves with good people, and this way not only do they enhance and ensure their own security but also, if they find themselves lost or misdirected, their cohorts will help them.

This dvar Torah contains an invaluable piece of advice within it. When you feel that your staff is cast down and that perhaps you are surrounded by the wrong influences, remember that you can always grasp the snake's tail, and it will become a staff in your palm once again. There are times when you need to return to what will strengthen your observance. When you come home for Shabbat, use some of the time to recharge your batteries, engage and learn with your friends in the

---

60   Exodus 7:9.
61   Exodus 4:4.

neighborhood who are attending yeshivot, learn for a few minutes with me, attend minyan at least when you are home, and if you have a *regilah* (time off from the army), it's a good time to stop by your *mechinah*. The effort should give you strength to overcome some of the challenges that you might experience in the army.

> ▸ *I appreciate the advice and your words, but as you know, to learn Torah and even go to minyan requires desire and effort. I am so busy during the week and pushed in so many directions that by the time I get home and can finally rest and chill, that effort and desire is just burned out. I am also aware that you want me to stay strong, and particularly when I am home to commit myself to things. Believe me, deep down it is something that I want as well, but please respect not only how difficult it is for me during the week but also what a relief it is for me when I get home not to have to follow orders, or just to have down time in which I decide for myself what I want to do.*

Yes, I have to be understanding of your predicament, which is difficult to do or to fully appreciate because I am not the one going through it. However, I also feel that I have to encourage you in some form or fashion to stay focused and committed, not only for the here and now but also for the future. I will do my best to remember what you're telling me, and please try your best to consider my advice.

> ▸ *OK, that sounds fair, but please don't get overly disappointed if I do not or I cannot; it is nothing personal against you, and I don't appreciate when you are too forceful or overbearing, especially when I need space.*

Fair enough, I will certainly try as well.

Bo

January 10, 2016

Yakov,

Parashat Bo is special for us, as it is your bar mitzvah *parashah* as well as mine and your brother Yisrael's as well, and it opens with "Come to Pharaoh."[62]

Grammatically the opening word is strange; what it should have said was "go" to Pharaoh, as opposed to "come" to Pharaoh.

The Kotzker Rebbe explains that for someone who is convinced that Hashem is always with him and by his side, the word *come* makes perfect sense. Hashem was inviting Moshe to "come" with him to Pharaoh; therefore the words "Come to Pharaoh" indicate that a believer will understand that Hashem is consistently with him.

I thoroughly enjoyed being together this Shabbat, and I apologize I did not take enough time to learn with you and to schmooze with you more; I look forward to the next Shabbat together soon, God willing.

> ▶ *There is no need to apologize, Abba; I enjoy our time and my time at home, and even when we are not conversing directly, just being around you and the family is comforting and rejuvenating. Miss you a lot and wish you shavua tov (a good week).*

---

62   Exodus 10:1.

January 15, 2016

Good morning.

In the middle of Parashat Bo, we are told that "the man Moses was very great in the land of Egypt, in the sight of Pharaoh's servants, and in the sight of the people."[63]

Many leaders, particularly those who govern nations, forget about their people. Rarely does one find a leader who commands respect while showing sincere concern for the people around him. The Torah confirms that Moshe commanded respect, as it says he was "very great in the land of Egypt," but he also knew how to relate to the people around him, as it says he was great "in the sight of Pharaoh's servants and in the sight of the people."

Following the sin of the Golden Calf, Hashem instructed Moshe, "Go descend"[64] to the Jewish people; this was not simply a physical directive. Hashem told Moshe that he must "descend" from his authoritative position and spiritual heights in order to speak to the people on a level they could comprehend. This was the only way to inspire them to reawaken their rapport with Hashem, as the Gemara demands of a leader to be "considerate and sensitive to the opinions of those around you."

The greatest leader commands the respect of others because of the respect he shows to those around him, particularly those who may feel inferior because of his position and stature.

May Hashem help you reveal your attributes of leadership through your service, and may you continue to relate with understanding to all those around you, and consequently earn the respect of your peers and superiors.

Shabbat shalom.

---

63   Exodus 11:3.
64   Exodus 32:7.

► *I have to say that, while there is a chain of command in the army which obviously has to be followed, even our officers demonstrate sensitivity and friendship at times. They do maintain a distance from us, but every once in a while we get a glimpse that they are human and that we are all trying to achieve the same goals.*

Shabbat shalom.

Beshalach

January 18, 2016

Yakov,

The Torah introduces the song that Bnei Yisrael sang following the parting of the Reed Sea as follows: "and the people feared the Lord, and they believed in the Lord and in His servant Moses. Then sang Moses and the children of Israel this song to the Lord."[65]

The Degel Machaneh Ephraim points out that the *pasuk* affirms, "Then sang Moses and the children of Israel"; Moshe was first to sing, and Bnei Yisrael joined in. Why? He explains that prior to the song, the Torah says that Bnei Yisrael "believed in the Lord and in His servant Moses"; Moshe felt that Bnei Yisrael supported him and his connection with Hashem. Knowing that he had the support of the people he was leading was reason enough for Moshe to sing.

▸ *This is precisely why I went to* mechinah *before the army; they concentrated on topics of* emunah *(faith), leadership, and character development. One of the things they emphasized is what you are expressing in your* dvar Torah: *a leader is most effective when he recognizes that his people believe in his capabilities and mission. I hope to put what I learned to good use, not only in the army but also in general. By the way, while we are talking about leadership, happy birthday; I couldn't ask for a better father. I love you, and may you live in good health to 120.*

---

65 Exodus 14:31, 15:1.

January 22, 2016

Boker tov (good morning).

When the Jewish people reach the Reed Sea and need salvation, Moshe tells them, "The Lord will fight for you, and you shall hold your peace."[66]

Yet when they are faced with confronting Amalek, their sworn enemy, Moshe tells Yehoshua, "Choose for us men, and go out, fight with Amalek."[67]

Why is it that at the Reed Sea Bnei Yisrael are reassured that "The Lord will fight for you," but regarding Amalek, Moshe must ensure that Yehoshua amasses an army for battle?

When Am Yisrael first came out of Egypt and were confronted with the Reed Sea in front of them and the Egyptian legion behind, they were not yet prepared to defend themselves. For this reason Moshe encouraged them by reminding them of Hashem's constant vigil and assistance: "The Lord will fight for you." However at some point Am Yisrael would have to invest in their own salvation. The Torah wants us to remember that Hashem helps those who help themselves; even though we must rely on Hashem's salvation, that should not become habitual. We as a people have to "go out [and] fight" and bear arms in order to create our own salvation, with Hashem's help.

You bear both arms and tefillin, which shows your deep faith in Hashem and your preparedness to engage and defend.

---

66   Exodus 14:14.
67   Exodus 17:9.

Yitro

January 25, 2016

Good morning, Yakov.

Yitro is introduced by the Torah for the first time as "Jethro, the priest of Midian, Moses' father-in-law."[68] However, the second time he is described exclusively as "Jethro, Moses' father-in-law."[69]

The Ohr Hachayim explains that, although Yitro held the important title of "priest of Midian," he chose to be referred to as "Moses' father-in-law." He felt that the greatest title and honor was to be associated with his son-in-law, Moshe. He understood the importance of associating with great people, and the fact that Moshe was a prophet who was so close to Hashem made Yitro proud.

This reminds me of Zadie (Grandfather), because many times when I am with him and he meets a friend or someone he knows, he will say, "This is my son Shalom, who does the following…"; Zadie chooses to be remembered and distinguished by his children and grandchildren. He understands that the legacy he bore can only be actualized through future generations.

Yakov, it is a blessing to be connected with your parents, but even more when your family and friends are proud to be connected with you. We know it is difficult for you in the army, which is why it is important for you to remember that wherever we go, we proudly declare, "This is our son Yakov, who serves in the Israeli army."

Abba

---

68   Exodus 18:1.
69   Exodus 18:2.

▶ *Thank you very much, Abba, very nice, but it is important for you to know that I do not find the army difficult; I find it challenging, and there is a difference. Someone who finds his job "difficult" is a complainer, and he might as well give up before he's started, but to find your job "challenging" is a great thing, because challenges encourage growth and lead to greatness. I think this is why it is important to distinguish. Eretz Yisrael is not a "difficult" land, but it is a land that knows many "challenges." This is why Tzahal is the greatest army which protects the greatest land and the greatest people.*

I always tell Americans who make aliyah that they do not become full-fledged Israelis until they see their first child drafted into the army. While that moment makes people anxious, it is also a moment of tremendous pride and gratification. What you have written above makes us very proud, and instills within us confidence that living in Israel and sending you to the army is the most correct decision we have made.

January 29, 2016

Bnei Yisrael were instructed to prepare themselves for two days in order to receive the Torah, as the Torah says, "And the Lord said to Moses, 'Go to the people, and sanctify them today and tomorrow....'"[70]

The Pardes Yosef comments that the preparations were over a two-day period, representing the need to prepare both prior to receiving the Torah and after it was accepted. He explains that the real challenge for accepting the Torah is not when one is next to Har Sinai in the direct presence of the Spirit of Hashem, but rather when one leaves Har Sinai.

There is a famous story about the Gaon of Vilna, who would go to the Dubno Maggid once a year to receive constructive criticism. What can one possibly tell the Gaon? Apparently (or at least as legend would have it) the Maggid would tell him that it is quite some feat to become the Gaon in the confines of a yeshiva, but the test is to become the Gaon even outside the confines of the yeshiva.

Yakov, to be a committed Jew within the walls of a yeshiva and the confines of a shul – next to Har Sinai, as it were – is not as difficult as remaining committed when you leave these spiritual homes. Tomorrow you go out to the field, away from base and shelter. Both physically and spiritually you have the opportunity to "sanctify tomorrow" and make a *kiddush Hashem* based on what you have sanctified today.

► *Nice thought; however, I look at things differently. To me the very essence of Tzahal is holy, and therefore I am not going "out to sanctify"; rather, the meaning of my service and being part of an institution that is itself holy is the greatest sign of a spiritual existence.*

---

70   Exodus 19:10.

Rashi addresses the connection between the conclusion of Parashat Yitro, which describes the construction of the stone Altar, and the beginning of Parashat Mishpatim, which opens, "Now these are the ordinances which you shall set before them."[71]

He explains that the Sanhedrin in Jerusalem that maintains enactment of the ordinances must sit where the Altar is, in the heart of the Temple, signifying that the purpose of the Temple and the Altar is to endorse performance of the ordinances and laws of the Torah. I am very impressed with the fact that you see the entire institution of Tzahal as a Temple, but remember that a Temple is not holy in and of itself; it is only sacred when run in accordance with the laws of the Torah and for the purpose of disseminating them, and the same goes for the army.

Remember, all of us need the means and tools with which to create holiness. Tzahal is a "holy" institution because it enables us to fulfill a mitzvah from the Torah, to conquer and settle our land. Ultimately, we need the mitzvot of the Torah to reveal how to create more holiness and spiritual bodies in the material world in which we live.

In the middle of the *parashah*, the Torah commands, "And you shall be holy people to Me; therefore you shall not eat any flesh that is torn of beasts in the field."[72]

Man's purpose in this world is to sanctify the mundane world around him, which is challenging. Perhaps this is why we are told to be "holy people" within the same *pasuk* that reminds us not to "eat any flesh that is torn of beasts in the field." We are expected to sanctify ourselves even when we are involved in the most basic functions such as eating, because that is what makes us "holy people."

I know and understand that the army is a holy institution because of the mitzvot one fulfills when he serves in it, but it is easy to lose sight of that perspective, particularly when your day-to-day tasks in the army are so physical by nature.

---

71   Exodus 21:1.
72   Exodus 22:30.

Mishpatim

February 4, 2016

Hi, Yakov.

Here is a story that happened to me last night when I was speaking at a shul here in America. I mentioned that in the middle of the *parashah*, the Torah relates the importance of lending money and helping poor people: "If you lend money...to the poor person who is with you, you shall not be to him as a creditor; neither shall you lay upon him interest."[73]

Some explain that the phrase "the poor person who is with you" is referring to the poor person himself, and the Torah is warning that even the destitute must look after other poor people, and they too must not act toward others "as a creditor." After I shared this comment, a fellow came to me excitedly and told me that he once saw his grandmother give a needy fellow a few packages of food. He asked his grandmother why she was packing away so much food for one poor person when they did not have much to eat for themselves. The grandmother responded that she was not only providing food for this unfortunate fellow, but she was also giving him enough so that if other poor people approached him, he could help provide for them. It is an amazing and beautiful thing to see how the Jewish people show concern for one another.

▶ *That is a nice story. I find that one thing all Jewish people can relate to, even if we are not always so good at it, is the concept of man's treatment of his fellow man. There are many guys in my unit who do not believe in God, but they are always supportive when it comes to respecting and helping one another.*

---

73   Exodus 22:24.

This is why the first half of Parashat Mishpatim consists of *mitzvot bein adam l'chavero* (commandments [regarding behavior] between man and his fellow man), and only after that does the Torah address our relationship with Hashem, because before someone tries to establish rapport with Hashem, Who is beyond comprehension, he first has to know how to relate to his fellow man, who is accessible. Yet the *mitzvot bein adam la'Makom* (commandments [regarding behavior] between man and God) do indeed follow the *mitzvot bein adam l'chavero*, because one set is meant to lead us to the other.

I often hear from nonobservant people that they feel they do not need to fulfill *mitzvot bein adam la'Makom* because they fulfill their duties in more important places such as the *mitzvot bein adam l'chavero*. To me this represents an unwillingness to confront a greater spiritual obligation toward Hashem, Who is obviously more foreign and difficult to deal with.

▶ *Abba, I am not trying to find excuses for people who do not believe in Hashem, I am just telling you the facts. I think if they cannot keep the* mitzvot bein adam la'Makom, *it is nonetheless commendable that they feel a need and a connection to what we call* mitzvot bein adam l'chavero, *which they seem to have. This is a good thing because at least there is some connection and affiliation to part of their Jewishness.*

Terumah

February 9, 2016

Parashat Terumah describes the construction of the Tabernacle and the vessels and utensils that adorned it. The Holy Ark was the central utensil in the Tabernacle. The Torah instructs: "And you shall put the staves into the rings on the sides of the Ark, with which to carry the Ark. The staves shall remain in the rings of the Ark; they shall not be removed from it."[74]

The *Meshech Chochmah* explains that the Ark held the tablets, representing the Torah. The staves that carried the Ark could never be removed, representing the preparedness that Am Yisrael needed to carry the Torah with them throughout their travels. No matter where they found themselves, it was essential that Am Yisrael take the Torah.

This message describes your mission as well. Take the Torah with you when you are on base, when you are out in the fields, when you are in the middle of a training exercise, so long as the Torah is by your side and "the staves shall remain in the rings of the Ark," you will be secure.

▶ *Thanks; to tell you the truth now I appreciate a little more what we say in the Shema every day, "Teach them diligently to your children, and talk of them...when you walk by the way."[75] It is quite challenging to learn or even concentrate on learning something when you are walking by the way, or I guess in my situation running from place to place is a more accurate description. Having your divrei Torah on my phone when I have a few moments to read them really helps to fulfill this directive, so thank you for helping me with this.*

---

74 Exodus 25:14, 15.
75 Deuteronomy 6:7.

Tetzaveh

February 16, 2016

The only oil that could be used to light the Menorah in the Mishkan (Tabernacle) as well as in the Batei Hamikdash was pure pressed olive oil, as the verse states, "And you shall command the Children of Israel that they bring for you pure pressed olive oil for the light, to cause a lamp to burn continually."[76] Why is it that the oil had to be "pure pressed"?

Perhaps the Torah is teaching us an important lesson. Illuminating and purifying one's surroundings through ideology and a spiritual purpose such as Torah and mitzvot requires earnestness and sacrifice. One must invest and expend energies much as is done when one has to press and crush an olive in order to squeeze the desired virgin olive oil.

This concept is confirmed in the Gemara, which states, "And Rabbi Yitzchak says, 'If a person says to you…I have invested and succeeded, then believe him.'"[77]

All things that are altruistically worthwhile require our uncompromised determination; thank you for offering yours.

Abba

---

76   Exodus 27:20.
77   Babylonian Talmud, *Megillah* 6b.

Ki Tisa

February 24, 2016

Good morning, Yakov.

Following the sin of the Golden Calf, Moshe said to Hashem, "Oh, this people have sinned a great sin."[78]

Why refer to the sin as "great," which only calls more attention to the sin and would appear to make matters worse?

Repentance begins with confession and the ability to recognize that the act was wrong. Moshe told Hashem that the sin Bnei Yisrael transgressed was "great," thereby admitting and revealing the nature of the sin, unlike Adam who, when confronted by Hashem regarding his having eaten from the tree of knowledge said, "The woman whom You gave to be with me, she gave me of the tree, and I ate."[79] Adam avoided responsibility, precisely what Moshe wanted to correct.

Leadership begins with the ability to recognize that mistakes can be made, and we are only human after all.

---

78 Exodus 32:31.
79 Genesis 3:12.

February 25, 2016

Good morning, Yakov.

Following the sin of the Golden Calf, Moshe asked of Hashem, "Show me, I pray, Your glory."[80]

Hashem responded, "and you will see My back, but My face shall not be seen."[81]

The Torat Moshe explains that Hashem's response was symbolic. Hashem told Moshe, "and you will see My back," reminding him that man is limited. As events unfurl in the world, it is difficult for us to understand them, and only at times in hindsight we can comprehend why Hashem did what He did. However, regarding seeing the future or even at times grasping the present, Hashem says, "but My face shall not be seen." This response describes the events and happenings that only Hashem knows.

It is important for us to remember, particularly when things are challenging, that most of the time we are incapable of seeing the full picture and, although it is difficult to do so, we should remember that ultimately Hashem not only comprehends but also creates the full picture and oversees the game plan.

Hang in there,

Abba

▶ *Very true. When things get difficult, my spirit can become downcast and sometimes I even ask myself why exactly I am going through this, but thinking of ideology, religion, and yes, Hashem, is helpful.*

---

80   Exodus 33:18.
81   Exodus 33:23.

March 16, 2017

▸ *Abba! I wanted to wish you good luck for the marathon. Have a great and amazing time.*

Enjoy every single moment of the run, even the hard parts. Remember that for two thousand years we weren't able to run in our own country and especially in Yerushalayim; there is no better place in the world for your legs to hurt than in Yerushalayim.

Your first marathon only happens once, and remember that in the end, everything finishes. Love you so much, and I will meet you at 21K!

Good luck.

Wow! That is a beautiful thought, Yakov, and thanks for thinking of me. Look forward to seeing you at 21K; it will certainly help me out.

Vayakhel

March 4, 2016

Good morning, Yakov.
The Mishkan is referred to as Mishkan Ha'edut, the Tabernacle that testifies; what does this mean?

The *Meshech Chochmah* explains the meaning based on the Tosefta, which says, "If the Tabernacle is properly constructed but the Aron is not placed within its confines, then it is just a large edifice."

The Mishkan derives its holiness and purpose from the Ark and the Torah that rests within it. Therefore, the Tabernacle "testifies" that the only reason it reveals the Divine Spirit of Hashem is because of the Torah that rests within it, without which it would hold no significance.

Each and every one of us represents a Tabernacle, and the question is what do we put inside this Tabernacle called ourselves? While you are and inevitably will be confronted with hardships in the army, use this wonderful opportunity to "construct your Tabernacle," so that one day it will serve as a means of "testifying" to all that happens when you allow greatness to reside within.

With love and admiration,
Abba

▶ *Thanks, Abba, that is really nice. I will be home in about two hours.*

Pekudei

March 9, 2016

With the completion of the construction of the Mishkan, the Torah says, "And it came to pass in the first month in the second year, on the first day of the month, that the Tabernacle was erected. And Moses erected the Tabernacle."[82]

What is the significance of emphasizing that "Moses erected the Tabernacle" once the Torah already confirmed that "the Tabernacle was erected"?

When the Torah says that "the Tabernacle was erected," it confirms that the physical materials and utensils used within the Tabernacle were now completed, but their spiritual usage had not yet been revealed. Moshe then instructed Bnei Yisrael how to take the utensils and infuse them with meaning by demonstrating how to use each one to serve Hashem within the Tabernacle. The Torah therefore credits Moshe with "erecting the Tabernacle" because he took the materials of "the Tabernacle [that] was erected" and sanctified them by revealing their spiritual purpose.

I suppose this is our job in the world. We have to demonstrate how everything, including that which appears mundane and insignificant, can be used for greater purpose.

---

82   Exodus 40:17–18.

Vayikra

March 15, 2016

Good morning, Yakov.

There are three primary reasons that an animal called a *beheimah* can be offered as a sacrifice, as opposed to an animal called a *chayah*, which is prohibited.

One reason given is that a *beheimah* is easier to catch, making it readily available and more convenient to offer as a sacrifice. Secondly, the *chayah* is considered arrogant and aggressive due to its nature, which is to hunt other animals. Finally, the *beheimah* is typically hunted by the *chayah*, and symbolically, Hashem prefers to receive and embrace the hunted as opposed to the hunter.

These three reasons reflect a certain approach we should have in the way we conduct our lives. We too are expected to be readily available when it comes to serving Hashem, and when the occasion presents itself to fulfill a mitzvah we should respond without hesitation.

In addition, we need to recognize that modesty will sensitize us to the needs of our fellow man and certainly to our responsibilities to Hashem.

Finally, while we need to protect ourselves from harm and from our enemies, we should consistently strive to make peace and to avoid being the aggressor as much as possible. I believe these attributes are enlightening regarding Tzahal as well.

The army offers consistent opportunities to serve Hashem and His people. Even if you cannot open a *sefer* to learn or you do not have the time to daven properly with a minyan, your protecting the Jewish people and securing the boundaries of Eretz Yisrael is itself a constant means of serving Hashem and heeding His call. Serving in Tzahal should promote the thought that in the end we are all human, and without

Hashem's help we could not succeed, as the *navi* says, "Not by might, nor by power, but by My spirit, says the Lord of hosts."[83]

Tzahal is also an army that defends its country and people, while upholding humanitarian values and the sanctity of life.

We should be privileged to see the fulfillment of the prophecy "and the lion shall eat straw like the ox."[84]

Abba

▶ *Tzahal is an army that tries to be humanitarian and this is something that we discuss a lot in the army, but it is also very difficult to incorporate; at the end of the day, no matter how compassionate you think you are or you try to be, it is difficult for an army to maintain compassion when it also needs to be aggressive in order to secure our people and land. We are given instructions however in the army to do the best we can. For example, we are taught about the IDF ethics code and "purity of arms." As you know, these terms refer to ethical standards in the army and how our ammunition is to be used only to complete a mission, in defense of civilians, and that we are expected to do everything possible to avoid harming other civilians and their property. However, it gets tricky at times. For example, just now when we were in Hebron, we caught a terrorist (thank God before he perpetrated his attack) and brought him back to base before he was taken off for interrogation by a different unit. The night we brought the terrorist in was chilly. He was not covered enough and was obviously very cold. One of the guys gave him his coat to help him stay warm, and we were fine with that and understanding, but then this*

---

83   Zechariah 4:6.
84   Isaiah 11:7.

same guy wanted to give this terrorist a bed to sleep in, and most of us felt that was not only uncalled for but also inappropriate. After all, this guy is a terrorist and would have killed any one of us and any Israeli civilian if he had the chance; why would we offer him such comfort? In other words, I, and I think most of my colleagues, understood the need to cover him with a coat because it is inhumane to leave someone (even a terrorist) shivering from the cold, but I think you cross the line when you offer him a bed to sleep in. This becomes self-defeatist, disrespectful, and even detrimental to our efforts as chayalei Tzahal.

Bottom line, everything is relative, particularly with regard to these obscure and unclear parameters.

Your predicament is indeed a very challenging one, and in fact it is expressed in the Midrash with regard to Shaul Hamelech. Shaul was instructed very clearly by Shmuel to smite Amalek and to confiscate all that is theirs. He nevertheless spared Agag the king of Amalek and many others, including the women and children, to which the Midrash comments, "Rabbi Elazar said: One who becomes compassionate to the cruel will ultimately become cruel to the compassionate, as it is written, 'And Shaul and the nation spared Agag and the best sheep and cattle.'"[85]

While it is easy for us to defend Shaul's reasoning, particularly his unwillingness to harm the women and children of Amalek, he is nonetheless criticized for having ignored Hashem's directive, to the extent that ultimately he lost his right to be king.

You are describing very serious matters and you are right, it is difficult for Tzahal to define and clarify because no matter what you do when it comes to an army or to combat, it is challenging to deal with what is humane and how to maintain compassion toward others, even

---

85   I Samuel 15:9, cited in Midrash, *Ecclesiastes Rabbah* 7:16.

your enemies, despite war and confrontation. You also have to remember that no matter what we do and regardless of the standards we try to maintain, the world sees us as they wish, usually from a tainted perspective prone to criticism. You recall how during Operation Cast Lead, a BBC reporter contacted me to comment on her comparison of military rabbis going out with combat soldiers in the field to encourage troops before they fought to radical Islamic imams inciting terror attacks. The comparison is obviously absurd, which is why I immediately told the reporter I was not interested in conversing (this was the BBC, after all), and you and I know very well that the reason rabbis accompanied combat soldiers was that in case God forbid there were deaths (which was expected), they would be able to ensure that all bodies and body parts would be buried properly. Yet regardless of what we say or how we explain ourselves, it falls on deaf ears, which is why we have to try our best to maintain standards of ethics for our own conscience – but certainly not at any price.

The Torah regulates certain activities particularly during wartime to help us maintain sensitivity. For example, the Torah says, "When you besiege a city for a long time, in making war against it to take it, you shall not destroy its trees by wielding an axe against them, for you may eat of them, and you shall not cut them down…"[86] Specifically during wartime, the Torah asks us to sympathize with our surroundings in order to keep us civilized.

Another example is how the Torah instructs Bnei Yisrael to maintain cleanliness within the confines of an army camp: "You shall have a shovel in addition to your weapons, and it shall be that when you sit outside, you shall dig with it; you shall go back and cover that which comes from you. For the Lord your God walks in the midst of your camp."[87]

We are expected to cover our excrement within our camp during war because that is when people have a tendency to become more

86 Deuteronomy 20:19.
87 Deuteronomy 23:14, 15.

brutal or animalistic, and the Torah expects us to behave otherwise toward our fellow man and surroundings. These are principles and concepts that we subscribe to wholeheartedly, and they should be embedded within us. Yet we have to maintain a balance because there are limitations to being humanitarian, particularly in life-threatening situations, and the Torah offers an insightful guideline for this as well.

When Rivkah meets Eliezer at the well, she offers him water and gives him to drink; following his drinking the Torah says, "And when she had finished giving him drink, she said, 'I will draw for your camels also, until they have finished drinking.'"[88]

It is difficult to understand why Rivkah gave water to Eliezer first when we know that there is a rule in the Talmud that states, "Rabbi Yehuda in the name of Rav said: it is prohibited for someone to feed himself before feeding his animals, as it says: 'I will provide grass in your field for your cattle and you will eat and be satisfied.' First it says, 'I will provide grass in your field for your cattle,' and only after does it say, 'and you will eat and be satisfied.'"[89]

Why then did Rivkah give water to Eliezer first?

The Talmud says one cannot *feed* himself before the animals, referring to food, but with regard to water, a bare necessity and a basic for survival, man comes before his animals. In other words, we are expected to be sensitive and caring, but not at the expense of our own lives, which is why with regard to drinking water a person takes before his animals. This same concept should be applied to the situation you were in, which in my opinion was handled correctly. Perhaps we should even cover a terrorist who is cold, if only to maintain our human dignity in the face of hostility, but offering a bed transmits the wrong message, and I think letting one's guard down to that extent can endanger your security. Of course, when you are confronted with these quandaries that require immediate response, it is not easy to make cool calculations.

---

88 Genesis 24:19.
89 Babylonian Talmud, *Berachot* 40a.

March 16, 2016

The first sacrifice introduced by the Torah is the *korban olah* (burnt offering), of which the Torah says, "you [plural] shall bring your offering."[90] Rashi comments on this, "From here we learn that the *olah* sacrifice may be offered by two people at once as a partnership."

The Yismach Yisrael says that Rashi's emphasis on offering the *olah* in unison is fitting, considering that the word *olah* means "to spiritually raise." Unity is conducive to sanctity. An example would be to pray with ten men in a minyan rather than by one's self, because the Presence of Hashem is felt more strongly within the group of ten.

Rabbeinu Bachye explains that the *olah* is the first sacrifice introduced in the Torah, based on the principle that says, "the end act is always based on the initial thought"; everything begins with one's thoughts. The *olah* is a sacrifice that atones for wayward thoughts, and for this reason the Torah begins with it, demonstrating that from the outset one's thoughts must be in order; only then can they translate into action.

---

90 Leviticus 1:2.

March 17, 2016

I saw a beautiful thought from the Chidushei Harim regarding the *korban olah*. Each type of *korban olah* introduced by the Torah concludes with the following statement: "…an elevation offering, a fire offering, a satisfying aroma to Hashem."[91]

An aroma that emanates from afar eventually wafts closer so that one can enjoy the smell; the same regarding the sacrificial offering. A sacrifice does not necessitate an immediate effect on a person, even if one is bringing the sacrifice to atone for his sins; rather it is supposed to remind a person that he should reconsider his behavior and adopt a new mode for the future. One may not appreciate the immediate effects of a sacrificial offering, but eventually, much like an aroma that reaches a person after a delay, the sacrifice is meant to have a long-term effect on his attitude and behavior.

When you recognize that you are securing not only the present but the future of the people and Land of Israel, then I believe it will be easier to overcome the various challenges you encounter in service.

Abba

▶ *Abba, I read your* dvar Torah, *and it was very nice. You always like to quote Rabbi Wein and say, "If we do not appreciate our past we cannot possibly secure our future"; I believe the army recognizes this as well. This is why we are provided with educational lectures and seminars to help us realize that we are part of a nation with a rich history and connection to Eretz Yisrael. As a religious person, obviously I feel a spiritual connection to Eretz Yisrael and Am Yisrael as well, but remember the army does not adopt that position, and many of the soldiers are secular and so that is foreign to them. In*

---

91 Leviticus 1:9.

fact, it is difficult at times to convince and demonstrate to many of the secular soldiers that even historically we have a right and connection to the land. Some of them are so indoctrinated, even as soldiers they are apologetic for the "Israeli occupation," which really upsets me. This is why it is important for all of us, particularly those who do not have a "religious" connection to the land, to value our relationship with Eretz Yisrael, at the very least from a cultural and historical perspective.

Hey, you are preaching to the choir. That is exactly why I started Makom Meshutaf, because many Israelis do not want to relate to Judaism at large from a religious perspective, so at the very least they need to be made aware of what Judaism and Israel have to offer from a historical and cultural one. Strange as this may sound, I happen to think this is a great learning experience for you as well, to be exposed to this reality of what we should and have to deal with in Israeli society constructively.

Shabbat shalom.

Purim

March 21, 2016

Boker tov.

This week's Torah portion of Tetzaveh introduces the esoteric concept of the *bigdei kehunah*, the clothing worn by the Kohanim while serving in the Mikdash. While these directives appear to be quite foreign, it is important to reveal the message they convey to us.

When Moshe is instructed to inform Aharon about the priestly garments he would wear in the Tabernacle, the Torah consistently stresses their purpose: "And you shall speak to all of the wise-hearted people whom I have filled with the spirit of wisdom, that they make Aharon's garments to sanctify him, that he may minister to Me in the priest's office."[92]

Perhaps the Torah wants us to understand that clothing can be elevated and used for a great purpose. A uniform can be both meaningful and useful, depending on who dons it and for what reason; it can represent a mission, when worn by the right person with the proper intentions.

The beginning of Megillat Esther reveals a girl not fully confident nor fully capable of fulfilling the mission she is given; this is evident by the fact that she is consistently told by Mordechai what to do. The Megillah relates Esther's transformation in the later chapters as it says, "Esther put on her royal apparel."[93]

This does not merely describe a physical motion; it suggests that Esther "donned the royal garments," surrounding herself with the Divine Presence, "to minister to Me," to fulfill her calling by serving Hashem and His people.

---

92   Exodus 28:3.
93   Esther 5:1.

In the same vein, Rashi comments, "The rabbis explain that she was adorned with the spirit of Hashem"[94]; what does this mean?

Rav Yakov Ariel explains that, while clothing is external, the person wearing the clothing can give it meaning. For example, a Kohen's garments must maintain purity because of the functions they serve for the Kohen to serve Hashem in the Temple. A soldier's uniform represents his preparedness to serve his people, which should make him feel honored and proud. When Esther put on her royal garb, she understood that she was placed in the position to serve as queen of Persia, to fulfill Hashem's mission by saving the Jewish nation from Haman. This is what the rabbis meant when they said that when she wore her royal garb, "she was adorned with the spirit of Hashem," because she understood that the reason she was wearing the clothing was solely to serve Hashem.

Interestingly, after Mordechai finds out about the evil decree of Haman and Achashverosh to destroy the Jewish people, he dresses in ashes and sackcloth. Esther sends him clothing to wear, but he rejects the clothing and says to her, "Do not imagine that you shall escape in the king's palace any more than the rest of the Jews. For if you hold your peace at this time, relief and deliverance will come to the Jews from some other place, but you and your father's house will perish; and who knows whether you did not come to royalty for such a time as this?"[95]

Mordechai reminded Esther that every day upon waking up in the wealth and splendor of Ahashverosh's palace and putting on her royal garb, she should ask herself "whether you did not come to royalty for such a time as this." A person who dons a uniform must remember its purpose.

You cannot join us for *seudat Purim* (the Purim meal) because you have a uniform to wear. Your uniform gives you the right to influence and secure the Land of Israel, "and who knows whether you did not come to royalty for such a time as this!"

94 Rashi, Esther 5:1.
95 Esther 4:13, 14.

One who wears a uniform, be it rabbinic garb or a soldier's fatigues, must recognize the message and image it transmits.

There is an additional message in the priestly garments regarding Jewish leadership and responsibility. When the Kohen left the confines of the Mikdash, he was required to remove the special garments. While no doubt this requirement contains many halachic parameters, such as the care the Kohen must take that his garments avoid becoming impure, it was also a means for the Kohanim to transmit a message to the nation. As a leader and rabbinic figure, the Kohen would remove his garments, thereby announcing that he is now grounded and available for consultation.

These two guidelines help ensure that sincerity would remain intact within the institution of Jewish leadership. As a *chayal*, you are a Jewish leader and conduct yourself appropriately. At the same time, you must be modest enough to communicate with the people you represent.

▶ *Very nice. Unfortunately, I think people relate to and respect* chayalim *today more than* rabbanim *(rabbis). I'm not sure if that says wonders about* chayalim *or negatives regarding* rabbanim. *Either way I am proud of my uniform and what it represents, and I try to remind myself every day of the responsibility that comes with wearing it.*

I agree with your assessment, and it's something I try to address. I like to refer to the Gemara in Shabbat which says that a *talmid chacham* (learned Torah scholar) who has a stain on his clothing is punishable by death.[96] Obviously the Gemara is not to be taken literally (we would not put someone to death for such an infraction), but it shows the seriousness of how a *talmid chacham* should present himself, particularly because he is in the public's eye. Someone who takes on a public

---

96 Babylonian Talmud, *Shabbat* 114a.

position is subject to deep scrutiny and therefore must take extra care regarding behavior and appearance. Unfortunately, that does not always happen, and at the end of the day people are human; even rabbis make mistakes and miscalculations or commit sins. Rabbi Wein always likes to say, "Don't judge Judaism by the Jews." I am glad that you feel the weight of responsibility when you wear your uniform and recognize the opportunity you have to exemplify sincere leadership to Am Yisrael, as should anyone who assumes a position of authority.

Tzav

March 22, 2016

Here is a really nice insight I saw. The Torah instructs, "Fire shall be kept burning on the Altar continually; it shall not go out."[97]

The Jerusalem Talmud comments on the latter directive in the verse, "it shall not be extinguished – even when traveling."[98]

What does this mean?

When a person is close to his home and familiar surroundings, generally speaking he is less likely to sin or behave out of the ordinary, perhaps because of his regimented schedule, or the concern of people close to him. However, when a person is far from home and the people who know him, that is when he is susceptible to temptation and can get into trouble, which is why it says in Psalms, "Happy is each person who fears the Lord, who walks in His ways."[99]

A person who truly fears Hashem is someone "who walks" and is traveling far from his place but remains "in His ways." Regardless of the environment he finds himself in, he remains steadfast and loyal to Hashem and His ordinances. This can help explain the meaning in the Talmud: "even when traveling" in unfamiliar terrain, one must ensure that the fire, representing commitment and dedication, like the sacrifice offered on the Altar, "shall not be extinguished."

At times like these, you have to ensure that "fire shall be kept burning on the Altar continually" and that "it shall not go out" even when you are moving from place to place during your service. Keep the fire that made an imprint on you during your life, and you will realize that "even when traveling," it cannot be extinguished.

---

97   Leviticus 6:6.
98   Babylonian Talmud, *Yoma* 4:6.
99   Psalms 128:1.

▸ *I wanted to tell you that last Shabbat the guys in the gedud (battalion) asked if there was a dvar Torah to say, and I gave over one of the divrei Torah you sent me.*

Wow, that is probably the greatest thing for me as a father to hear. Thank you for sharing that with me; did they like the *dvar Torah*?

▸ *Now you're pushing it...* ☺

▸ *Abba,*
   While it's tough to be here for Purim and not at the seudah with the family, I must say it was really nice that one of the rabbis from Machane Meshutaf in the Jewish Identity Branch in Tzahal came to read the Megillah for us. He also gave us food, and we managed to dance and sing a little, so we had a little taste of Purim. Please tell Machane Meshutaf that we really appreciate their work and help. Wanted to ask you: For mishloach manot (mandatory Purim gifts of food), how many people do I have to give to, and what should I give?

You should give two cooked, edible foods on which one says two different *berachot* (blessings) to two different friends. It is preferable if you can to give one directly and to the other through a *shaliach* (messenger); just appoint a friend as your *shaliach* and have him give the foods to someone else in your name.

▸ *What about matanot la'evyonim (charity for the poor)?*

You fulfill the mitzvah with whatever amount of charity you give, but the money has to be distributed on Purim day to poor people so it is available for them to use for their *seudat Purim*. You should probably give the money to the Machane Meshutaf rabbi who came by, and he can distribute the money wherever he lives, because you can't get the money to anyone off base. Although it is preferable that you perform the mitzvah yourself, if this is not an option, you are still reliant upon me as your father, and therefore I can fulfill the mitzvah for you as your *shaliach*, which is what I will do.

▶ *Ok, that is great. I won't have time or opportunity to eat the* seudah, *so if I just wash on some bread and eat something, is that ok?*

Yes, absolutely. *Purim sameach*, my friend. We will have you in mind, and I will make a *l'chaim* for you.

▶ Purim sameach...*send my love to everyone.*

Shemini

March 28, 2016

Following Aharon's sacrificial offering toward the dedication of the Mishkan, the Torah says that he immediately blessed the nation: "Aharon lifted up his hands toward the people, and blessed them,"[100] to which the Midrash comments, "At that moment [of Aharon's blessing], the priests merited the priestly gifts, and they merited the privilege of blessing the nation for generations to come."[101]

What is the meaning of this midrash?

The Shaarei Chaim explains that the priests were always reliant on the portions and gifts they received from the rest of the Jewish people, and if they were to consistently offer their blessings to the nation, it would appear as if they were doing so in the interest of receiving more gifts, which would have been highly inappropriate. Now that Aharon had blessed the people without any requirement or personal interest to do so, the rest of the priests would follow his example and avoid their own personal considerations, and this merit would facilitate their receiving priestly gifts and blessing the nation consistently.

The greatest type of service for Hashem and His people is one that is not linked with any personal advantage, as it says in *Pirkei Avot*, "Serve your Master (Hashem) unconditionally."[102]

Serving as a *chayal* in Tzahal is one of the greatest examples of serving Hashem unconditionally in the Jewish world today. May Hashem grant you only *berachot* in the merit of your dedication, and may you share those *berachot* with the nation around you, as the Kohanim were blessed to do through their service as well.

---

100 Leviticus 9:22.
101 Midrash, *Leviticus Rabbah* 9:22.
102 *Pirkei Avot* 1:3.

March 29, 2016

Boker tov.

Aharon's two sons Nadav and Avihu were consumed by fire following their offering of an alien fire in front of Hashem. Following their demise, the Torah records, "and Aharon was silent."[103]

The Midrash comments on Aharon's seemingly strange reaction: "How should Aharon have reacted? On the eighth day the flesh of the foreskin shall be circumcised."[104]

This Midrash's comment is very difficult to understand. What is the connection between the mitzvah of circumcision and Aharon's silence, and why should Aharon have mentioned something about the mitzvah of circumcision at the time?

A person is born uncircumcised because Hashem wants him to understand that he is incomplete and, while Hashem may have created him, he is expected to invest and contribute to complete both himself and the world around him by means of his actions, investments, and sometimes even sacrifice. This same principle applies regarding the obligation of the Kohanim to ignite the flame on the Altar. Although the fire from upon the Altar descended from the heavens, nonetheless the Talmud says, "It is a special mitzvah to light the fire."[105]

It is a mitzvah for the Kohanim to light the fire because they demonstrate their eagerness to reveal the Presence of Hashem in this world, and therefore the mitzvah of circumcision and lighting the fire on the Altar share the same purpose; both actions demonstrate a desire to complete and enhance the world.

Now we can understand the midrash. Aharon could have protested to Hashem by demanding that just as "on the eighth day the flesh of the foreskin shall be circumcised" and man participates in God's Creation,

---

103 Leviticus 10:3.
104 Midrash, *Leviticus Rabbah* 12.
105 Babylonian Talmud, *Eruvin* 63a.

so too his sons' intention for igniting the fire on the Altar was to contribute to God's sanctity in this world. Yet Aharon was silent. Why?

Aharon understood that there are times when man must simply watch and admire the greatness of Hashem and His works. The moment when the fire descended for the dedication of the Mishkan was such an instance. While Nadav and Avihu's intentions may have been good, their actions were inappropriate at a time reserved for revealing the greatness of Hashem, which is why the fire that they offered was called "strange fire."[106]

We can learn from this insight how important it is in life to have stability. While a person's intention to act and perform is commendable, there is no question that at times it must be restrained.

▶ *Practically speaking, in the army you really need a balance: when to be a "go getter" and when you are better leaving things alone. It's not easy to figure it out. You remember when I went to my commander and told him that I fell asleep while I was on guard duty. I told him that a lot of guys were falling asleep because we just did not have enough time to rest, and I wanted him to consider giving us more time to sleep; it is dangerous if we fall asleep on guard duty. In the end it didn't help anyone; he did not consider giving us more rest, and he punished me for sleeping on guard duty, even though it was by my own admission and no one ever caught me. It is tough to know what to do because on the one hand you want to be helpful, but on the other hand, if you are too determined you can mess yourself up. I know this is something that you emphasize to us very often, and I am sure what I experienced here is just one example of the way this test presents itself in life.*

---

106 Leviticus 10:1.

No doubt, so many successes in life are contingent upon balance, as you are seeing now and as you will see God willing in many areas of your life. A teacher has to find balance between friendship and disciplining. A parent must pick his battles, choosing when and how to say things to his children and when things are better left alone. A leader too must grapple with the extremes of closeness and distance he must maintain in his relationships. There is an interesting thought that I saw in the *parashah* which relates to this as well.

The Torah delineates the signs of a kosher animal: "Everything among the beasts that has a split hoof, which is completely cloven footed, and chews its cud – that you may eat."[107] Although it appears there is no reason for these parameters, the *Divrei Binah* explains that these restrictions represent practical guidelines on how one should lead his life.

Split hooves indicate that any steps a person takes in life should be calculated; he must evaluate both options in front of him to ensure the best chance of moving in the right direction. Chewing the cud signifies the ability to mull over an idea with consideration, once again to ensure that deliberate decisions are made.

This message is beneficial with regard to your service in Tzahal particularly when it comes to physical safety, but it also applies to any service we undertake in life. It is always crucial to evaluate everything we do and commit wholeheartedly. Someone told me that a good parent is someone whose actions reveal constant striving to be as close as possible to good. We make many mistakes and misjudgments along the way, but it is a learning experience in progress, nonetheless.

► *The* mechinah *prepared us for this and told us to find one or two mitzvot that we would fulfill consistently and never compromise on. For example, one may commit to put on tefillin regardless of the circumstance. Believe me,*

---

107 Leviticus 11:3.

there are times when it becomes challenging: if you are up all night guarding and you get back late in the day exhausted and limited in your time to rest, you can convince yourself to put on your tefillin later on in the day, and you must stick to it. Although one mitzvah may not appear to be a major accomplishment, it nonetheless feels good to adhere to the commitment, and it offers a sense of priority and promotes a connection you have nurtured through your own personal effort.

What is the mitzvah that you do not compromise on?

▶ *That's between me and Hashem.*

March 30, 2016

One of the nonkosher birds listed in the Torah is the *chasidah* (stork). Rashi explains that this bird is called *chasidah* because it performs acts of *chesed* (kindness) by ensuring that its species always has food. Rashi's explanation is difficult because according to the Ramban, birds listed as not kosher are unsympathetic by nature. Yet the *chasidah* is kind to its species, which negates the reasoning of the Ramban.

The Chidushei Harim explains that, even though the *chasidah* is kind to its fellows, it is not so regarding other birds; it is only concerned with the wellness of its own kind. From the Torah's perspective, that is considered cruel.

I thought how appropriate this is regarding Tzahal, an army predicated on morality; not only does it defend our nation, but it also attempts to preserve the lives of other nations. Contrary to popular belief, Tzahal tries to protect Palestinian citizens from harm as much as possible within the framework of conflict and combat; this is because the Jewish way has always been to promote the conservation of life.

This is why the Torah instructs, "When you besiege a city for a long time, in making war against it to take it, you shall not destroy its trees by wielding an axe against them, for you may eat of them, and you shall not cut them down..."[108]

This is also why the Gemara describes the Jewish nation as "merciful and sons of the merciful." In particular, when it comes to providing basic necessities such as food, we are expected to maintain the values of sustaining life. It is for this reason that Tzahal refers to itself as the "Israel Defense Forces," labeling itself as a defender.

Conclusively, one who values other people's lives enhances the value of his own life as well.

---

108 Deuteronomy 20:19.

Tazria

April 10, 2016

Chodesh tov.

I saw something over Shabbat that I wanted to share with you from Parashat Tazria.

After a woman gives birth, the Torah instructs, "she shall touch no sacred thing, nor come into the Sanctuary, until the completion of her days of purity."[109]

The Noam Elimelech explains that this verse reveals a lesson in spiritual development. Sincere spiritual growth is accomplished one step at a time. If a person wants to be close to Hashem and "enter the Sanctuary," he must do so through "completion of [the] days of purity" and move through stages of spiritual improvement.

I find that the best things in life usually do not arrive instantaneously but rather develop through a process, particularly in the area of spiritual development.

▶ *I am not sure in the framework of the army that we are going to spiritually develop; I think it is more about spiritual preservation. As I have said before, I imagine that if I stick to a mitzvah every day, that too is important.*

I understand. Just bear in mind that spiritual progress is not only about doing the same thing every day, which is part of it, but it is also about doing new things and finding different ways to reinforce your commitment. It is important not to become one-dimensional in all things in life.

---

109 Leviticus 12:4.

Metzora

April 14, 2016

There are a number of processes the *metzora* (one who is afflicted with *tzaraat* or biblical leprosy) has to go through in order to purify himself. One of them is upon the seventh day of separating himself from the rest of Bnei Yisrael, "...he shall shave all his hair off his head and his beard and his eyebrows, even all his hair shall he shave off..."[110]

If the Torah says that he is meant to shave off "all his hair," why does it also specify "off his head and his beard and his eyebrows"? This would seem to be superfluous.

The Kli Yakar explains that by delineating these three areas of the body, the Torah is accentuating why the person got leprosy to begin with. Chazal explain that leprosy results from three sins: haughtiness, speaking slander, and envy.[111] Therefore the leper shaves his head because that is where haughtiness stems from; his beard because that is the hair that surrounds his mouth, which is the source of slander; and his eyebrows because the eyes are what cause one to be envious.

All three of these sins of which a leper may be guilty are sins that originate in groups and in competitive situations. While undoubtably you are fulfilling a positive mitzvah serving in Tzahal, you must be careful at the same time in a large group and in a competitive environment such as the army to refrain from speaking improperly, thinking haughtily, and viewing others around you with envy.

---

110 Leviticus 14:9.
111 Babylonian Talmud, *Erchin* 16a.

Pesach

April 9, 2017

Toward the end of the Maggid section of the Haggadah, the text quotes the Mishnah: "Rabban Gamliel says anyone who does not iterate three subjects on Pesach does not fulfill his obligation [of the mitzvah to tell the story of Pesach], and these are: Pesach, matzah, and maror."[112]

The order of the three subjects which Rabban Gamliel lists does not make sense, because chronologically we should first speak about the maror, representing the bitter slavery that Bnei Yisrael experienced in Egypt; then address the matzah, which is the bread of affliction; and finally the Pesach, which was the lamb sacrifice offered to Hashem immediately prior to Bnei Yisrael's departure from Egypt.

There are many answers offered regarding this problem, but I would like to propose the following as it relates to your service in the army. This Mishnah is recited at the end of the Maggid (the main section which relates the story of our Exodus from Egypt). The Pesach is the sacrificial lamb that was offered to Hashem and whose blood was spread over the doorposts of every Jewish person's home prior to our leaving Egypt, and its message is significant. Bnei Yisrael is expected not only to reflect upon the past, but also to provide their own security and help actualize their future redemption together with Hashem. The lamb was considered a god to the Egyptians, and so when Bnei Yisrael took the lamb and slaughtered it in front of them, it was a means of demonstrating that we rely on Hashem for salvation, but we also understand it is important to take our redemption into our own hands. This is why we took the blood of the lamb and spread it across the doorpost, demonstrating that every Jewish home must play an active role in ensuring our

---

112 *Pesachim* 10:5.

freedom. Therefore, after having told the story of our slavery in Egypt, Rabban Gamliel lists the Pesach first, indicating that our redemption is up to us as well.

Another important perspective is offered by Rav Soloveitchik, who explains that the three entities of Pesach, matzah, and maror represent three institutions that combat the slave mentality and help us appreciate what it means to have liberty. A slave tries to forget his tormented past, and so we eat the maror, which reminds us of the bitter slavery in Egypt and brings us to reflect on our past, regardless of how painful it is. One who was enslaved longs for riches, which is why we eat the matzah to remind us that liberty cannot be bought but must be earned with intrinsic value. Finally, the slave tends to be self-centered; it is for this reason that we eat the Pesach sacrifice, which is consumed in a group, demonstrating the importance of unity, and focusing on a nation as opposed to one's self.

► *Today one of my friend's fathers came to base to visit, and he brought with him a lot of meat and fries. My friend's family is not observant, but he told me (without my asking) that the oven was left untouched for more than twenty-four hours. You think I can partake from the food? I'm afraid I know the answer, but I thought I might as well ask anyway.*

So sorry, Yakov, but you're correct; you know the answer already, and it is problematic on a number of counts. I respect the fact that you took the time to ask and clarify, as opposed to succumbing to your immediate desires (I am sure the food looks and tastes a lot better than the food you get on base). Sorry it cannot work out.

► *By the way, is it okay to eat matzah before Pesach? It is the only thing to eat here, because they made everything in this outpost kosher for Pesach already.*

It is no problem at all. The main time it is prohibited to eat matzah is on Erev Pesach; otherwise there are all different customs as to when you should refrain from eating matzah before Pesach. We refrain from eating matzah a month before, following Purim, but bear in mind this is just a custom, not a prohibition. I imagine this is why they have matzah already on base, although the army rabbi responsible for your area should remind everyone that they should not eat the matzah on Erev Pesach itself, and obviously the army should provide all of you with an alternative to eat. By the way, in case they do not, and you have nothing else to eat the day before Pesach, the Be'er Heitev says that you can even eat matzah on the night before Pesach, and only on the day of Erev Pesach would it be prohibited. Bear in mind that as a *chayal* you need to eat and have sustenance; otherwise we are talking about *pikuach nefesh* (preventing endangering one's life) as well as the lives of others.

April 10, 2017

Yakov,

I read a thought in one of your books by Rav Eli Sadan. I'm going to use it tonight, first night of Pesach, and I think it's a nice idea for you to share with the *chayalim* at the Seder this evening.

As you know, there are three mitzvot one can never transgress, according to the principle of *"yehareg v'al yaavor"* (one must allow himself to be killed rather than transgress). They are murder, idolatry, and a prohibited sexual relationship. All three of these mitzvot are negative wrongdoings, but there is one positive mitzvah to which *yehareg v'al yaavor* also applies, and that is the mitzvah of inheriting the Land of Israel, as the Torah says: "Behold, I have set the land before you; go in and possess the land which the Lord swore to your forefathers."[113]

While the Torah seems to instruct us to inherit Eretz Yisrael at any cost, there is also a directive in the Torah that seemingly contradicts this mitzvah, which requires us to preserve life at any cost, as it says, "You shall therefore keep My statutes and My ordinances, which if a man shall do, he shall live by them – I am the Lord."[114]

The Talmud learns from the words "he shall live by them" that we are required to prolong life; how then can the Torah instruct us to "possess the land" even at the expense of sacrificing one's life?

Rav Sadan explains, based on Rav Kook, that the concept of *pikuach nefesh docheh* (avoiding endangering one's life overrides everything) applies only when there is a threat to an individual's life, and he is personally in danger. However, this rule does not apply nationally. The nation of Israel cannot die, regardless of the challenges it confronts. The mitzvah of possessing the land is not a personal one, but rather communal and national. Since the Jewish nation cannot die, the concept of *pikuach nefesh* does not apply to this mitzvah, and one is obligated to possess the

---

113 Deuteronomy 1:8.
114 Leviticus 18:5.

Land of Israel regardless of the dangers involved in doing so. The concept of *Am Yisrael chai* (the Jewish people lives) obligates us to inherit the Land of Israel.

This theme really sums up Seder night. At the Pesach Seder we as a people and a nation boldly declare "*Am Yisrael chai*," the Jewish people lives regardless of countless attempts to destroy us. This is the approach one must adopt on Seder night and during the holiday of Pesach.

You *chayalim* are facilitators of the mitzvah to inherit the Land. You are the protectors who provide the Jewish nation the ability to proclaim "*Am Yisrael chai*" and ensure that we continue that proclamation for generations to come.

Please share this idea with your fellow soldiers at the Pesach Seder; I believe it will resonate with them and put Pesach into a perspective that they will appreciate.

▸ *Abba,*
  That is really nice. I would like to give that over at the Seder; I don't know when. It depends on which guarding shift I have. This is the first time I will not be with the family for the Seder.

I know, we will miss you.

▸ *I would like to share this with you and would ask that you share it with the rest of the family at the Seder.*
  The Mishnah says, "Ben Zoma explained it: It says, 'So that you remember the day you left Egypt all the days of your life.' Just 'the days of your life' would have referred to the days; 'all the days of your life' therefore refers to the nights as well."[115]

---

115 *Berachot* 1:5.

Ben Zoma is of the opinion that one must mention the exodus from Egypt even at night; he attributes importance to the nighttime. Nighttime is symbolic of difficult times in our history when we have had to struggle for survival, such as during the dark ages of the Spanish inquisition, during the reign of Communist Russia, or of course in Nazi Germany. It is during these challenging periods of history that a Jew might be afraid to reveal his Torah observance and therefore he may choose to celebrate his Passover Seder in hiding. What then is the value of mentioning our exodus from Egypt when we need to experience an exodus from the very predicament and dire situation we find ourselves in? How can we honestly proclaim that we are experiencing freedom? One might even assume that during such periods of trial and tribulation, we are exempt from telling over the story of yetziat Mitzrayim.

It is for this reason that Ben Zoma insightfully reminds us that "all the days of your life" includes "the nights as well," and even when we sit in darkness and experience persecution, we must relate and discuss the story of our exodus from Egypt. We must consistently be reminded of the fact that the Jewish people have experienced and will again experience redemption through the hand of Hashem.

We are truly blessed to be here in Eretz Yisrael and to know that we have our own Jewish army to secure our land; we merit witnessing the beginnings of the redemption of Am Yisrael. However, we must recognize that our redemption is unfortunately not complete. Last night I was in a meeting with my fellow sergeants in preparation for Pesach, and the entire meeting focused on the threat of an attack which would take place on Seder night and how prepared we must be should such an attack occur. There are still so many whose main interest is to threaten our existence, and the "night" of Ben Zoma has not yet morphed into "day"; yet that day is imminent. We must continue to have hope and faith in Hashem that He will save and redeem us. This is precisely why even in the army and in the middle of our military camp, we too will enact and experience the Pesach Seder in celebration of Chag Hacherut – the Holiday of our Liberty and Freedom. If and when we remember that "all the days of your life refers to the nights as well," then we have nothing to fear.

I would like to conclude with a speech that David Ben-Gurion gave regarding Pesach during a session in which he was discussing the establishment of Medinat Yisrael (the State of Israel) with his colleagues:

> More than 300 years ago a ship by the name of the Mayflower left Plymouth for the New World. It was a great event in American and English history. I wonder how many Englishmen or how many Americans know exactly the date when that ship left Plymouth, how many people were on the ship, and what was the kind of bread that people ate when they left Plymouth.
>
> Well, more than 3,300 years ago, the Jews left Egypt. It was more than 3,000 years ago and every Jew in the world knows exactly the date when we left. It was on the 15th of Nisan. The bread they ate was matzoth. Up to date all the Jews throughout the world on the 15th of Nisan eat the same matzoth, in America, in Russia, and tell the story of the [exodus] from Egypt and tell

what happened, all the sufferings that happened to the Jews since they went into exile. They finish by these two sentences: "This year we are slaves; next year we will be free. This year we are here; next year we will be in Zion, in the land of Israel." Jews are like that.[116]

This is the nature of the Jew. Chag Sameach. I love you all and will miss you.
   Yakov

---

116 David Ben-Gurion, statement, Public Hearing before the Anglo-American Committee of Inquiry, Jerusalem, March 11, 1936 (Jerusalem: Government Printing Office), http://cojs.org/wp-content/uploads/Public_Hearings_3.11.46.pdf.

April 14, 2017

Bnei Yisrael slaughtered a lamb for the Pesach sacrifice and spread its blood over their doorposts. This was a means of defaming the Egyptians' belief that the lamb was a god, and I think there is a very significant message in this service.

Egyptian culture was based on externalism. Chazal (our Sages of blessed memory) say that they were immersed in deviant sexual misconduct; they were enthralled by gold and silver, as evident by the burial of their kings in the pyramids with their treasures, and the very fact that they would call an animal a god indicates that they were incapable of dealing with the intangible and spiritual. Am Yisrael demonstrated that our beliefs are quite the opposite, based on internal and intrinsic spiritual meaning. This is why Am Yisrael was instructed to eat the *korban Pesach* (the Passover sacrifice) inside, without leaving the confines of their homes. This also may be why they spread the blood of the lamb over their doorposts. Spreading the blood on the doorpost and closing the door from the inside conveyed the message that our spirituality comes from within. This explains the mitzvah of mezuzah, and why we place it on our doorpost. As one enters his home, the mezuzah reminds him that everything inside the home comes from Hashem, and the way we serve Him is based on intrinsic ideals and not external appearances.

April 18, 2016

Good evening, Yakov.

Today I want to share something with you that happened to me just now as I was waiting to give a class on Pesach in Kibbutz Sde Boker. Believe it or not, they have a nice new small *beit knesset* (synagogue). When I arrived, I was welcomed by a lady from the kibbutz who coordinated the evening, and we noticed that the electricity in the *beit knesset* was not working. The lady called an electrician who lives on the kibbutz to fix the electricity, and when he was done, I asked him to stay for the class, to which he responded, "No, it is not really for me." I told him that we would be studying how to prepare properly for Pesach, and he reacted, "The only way I prepare for Pesach is by baking bread!"

I was not startled and told him that everyone has his own way of preparing for the holiday; this was his means of preparation. He responded that this was certainly something we could all agree on. When I told him that we probably agree on more things than he can imagine, he said that this was another thing he agreed with. Then we wished each other *Chag sameach*.

Once the electrician left, the lady, who had been listening to our exchange, said to me, "Don't you worry; he'll come to the next learning session. Believe me, he wouldn't have come to fix the electricity if he wasn't curious about Pesach."

In turn, I asserted that our dialogue could establish a rapport, and again she confirmed that indeed he would come to the next learning session.

You see, Yakov, it is so important to engage and speak with people. You never know what impact a conversation can have on the people you converse with, and this is precisely the idea of Pesach. The word divided into two segments means *peh sach* (mouth speaks). This holiday revolves around the importance of speaking with others, especially people from different backgrounds with opposing perspectives.

I think this is a good story you can tell over at the Pesach Seder to your fellow *chayalim*. While you may not see things the same way, you can sit and discuss things in a civilized, respectful, and productive way.

▶ *Good job; that is a really nice story and thought.*

April 19, 2016

Here is another story I want to share with you.

Last night I was in Kibbutz Gat for a Makom Meshutaf pre-Pesach program. We learned about the Pesach Seder and sang many of the songs. After the program, an elderly woman came over to me and said that she did not like Pesach for a long time. When I asked her why, she told me that she was born in Poland, and when she was five, her parents paid a Polish family to take her in as part of their family, in an attempt to save her from the Nazis. Unfortunately, she did not have the proper papers, and so she was passed from one family to another until she was just left in the middle of a certain town. As she stood in the town center, a dog started barking at her, and she ran into a food store. When the owner of the store asked her why she was by herself, she innocently explained that she was Jewish and her parents were killed; she just wanted something to eat. The store owner asked if she knew how to pray like a Christian, and when she said yes, she was handed over to the local Christian orphanage, where she was raised as a Christian child. She told me that to this day she remembers how they taught her in the school that the Jews used the blood of good Christian children to make their matzah.

Following the Holocaust, Yeshayahu Drucker, a Polish Jew who helped find hidden Jewish children, discovered she was Jewish and brought her to Eretz Yisrael. She grew up on Kibbutz Gat, where she lives to this day. She explained to me that she always associated Pesach with what she had been taught about the matzah, and she grew depressed upon seeing families sitting together at the Seder table, since her entire family had perished in the Holocaust. Nonetheless, she assured me that now she enjoys Pesach because she has been blessed with a family of her own, and her children and grandchildren now join her for the Pesach Seder.

To me this story is truly amazing because it substantiates what we recite from the Haggadah every year: "For in every single generation people rise up against us to annihilate us, and God saves us from their hands." That lady is living proof that it's true.

Perhaps this is also the meaning of a verse from Ezekiel which is also part of the Haggadah: "And when I passed by you and saw you wallowing in your blood, I said to you, 'In your blood you shall live!' I said to you, 'In your blood you shall live!'"[117]

This is the declaration we make when a child is circumcised, and it is a confirmation that Jewish blood that is shed is ultimately restored through future generations. This was the case with the woman in Kibbutz Gat, to the point where she is able to celebrate the holiday of Pesach again with her own extended Jewish family.

▸ *Wow! That is a pretty unbelievable story. It is also something I think all of us can relate to. Here we are in the army, still protecting Jewish lives. Even someone who does not believe in Hashem can at least recognize the miraculous nature of our existence, persecution after persecution. Eretz Yisrael has unified us as a people, and Medinat Yisrael has fortified us as a nation. I think that if someone comes to this type of recognition at the Seder, he has fulfilled his obligation of reciting the Pesach story, even if he may not have recited the text of the Haggadah, don't you?*

---

117 Ezekiel 16:6.

I most certainly agree. There is a reason that the biggest event in which the greatest number of Israelis, religious and nonobservant alike, participate is the Pesach Seder. I am sharing these thoughts and stories with you around Pesach time because while it may be difficult for you to know what to say at the Seder when you are mainly with secular guys, I think these stories can and should resonate with anyone in Israel, particularly with someone serving in the army. The moment they arrive at this basic recognition, they too should feel a part of the "Jewish story," and as you mentioned, they fulfill their obligation.

April 25, 2016

Good morning, Yakov.
Yesterday, Chol Hamoed Pesach (during the intermediary days of the Passover festival), I made a *siyum* (marked completion of learning) on Masechet (Tractate) *Niddah*. I am sorry you couldn't join us, but I wanted to share something I said.

The tractate concludes with the following insight, which we are all familiar with because we recite it every Shabbat after the Musaf service: "The academy of Eliyahu taught: He who studies Torah laws (*halachot*) every day has the assurance that he will be in the World to Come, as it says, 'The ways of the world are His' – do not read 'ways' but 'laws.'"[118]

Why does the *masechta* conclude with such a statement when it has nothing to do with the laws of family purity discussed in the entire tractate?

One answer is that, since *Niddah* is the last tractate of the entire Talmud, the rabbis didn't want people to feel that, since they had completed all of the Talmud, it was no longer necessary for them to learn or delve into the meaning of halachah; for this reason they offer a comment that promotes the need to immerse oneself consistently in the study of Torah laws every day.

---

118 Babylonian Talmud, *Niddah* 73a; *Megillah* 28b.

The Maharsha explains that, when it comes to family purity, people tend to be very stringent and automatically assume that a woman is impure even when she may not necessarily be according to halachah. While being extra stringent may appear to be something positive, it can also cause people to become lax in their studying these laws because they just apply stringencies without consideration for minute details. Therefore, the *masechta* concludes with the importance of knowing halachah in general, as if to encourage people to continue studying halachah even if people are rigid in a specific area. All the commentaries in answering this question emphasize the importance of both adhering to and studying comprehensive halachah, which brings to mind something I wanted to mention to you.

I was very happy when you called me yesterday after your patrol to ask how long one has during the course of the day to daven Musaf, and also whether the BBQ grill someone had on base could be kosher for Pesach. Your questions show that halachah is important to you and it is something to be proud of.

► *Thanks, Abba. I really don't think it was such a big deal; I just had those two questions to ask you, but I appreciate your seeing things that way. Mazal tov on your siyum, and I hope to be able to join you for future ones.*

April 26, 2016

Yesterday I quoted to you a discourse from Masechet Niddah, based on the verse in Habakkuk which says, "The ways of the world are His." This verse establishes how we are expected to believe that everything that happens in this world is from Hashem. The comment of the Talmud which says, "Do not read 'ways' but 'laws'" is, I believe, establishing both the importance of halachah and the need to walk in the ways of Hashem facilitated by halachah; hence the connection between "ways" and "laws."

We often discuss at home why so many young people are leaving Torah observance and, while there is no easy explanation and certainly no simple solution, I believe that there are two foundations a person needs in order to preserve his observance. The first is to know that Hashem influences the world and its "ways," and the second is to always look for new "ways" to incorporate significant "laws" and pertinent ideas into his life.

April 27, 2016

We are in the middle of Pesach, but I want to share with you something from Parashat Acharei Mot. At the beginning of the *parashah*, Hashem commands Moshe: "Speak to Aharon, your brother, that he not come at all times into the Sanctuary within the veil…that he not die.… With this shall Aharon come into the Sanctuary."[119]

It seems strange that the first *pasuk* prohibits Aharon from coming into the holy place and then immediately after the Torah instructs Aharon how to enter the holy place. Some commentaries explain that this is a lesson in life, and the first *pasuk* is preparation for the second. Only a person who feels that he may "not come at all times into the Sanctuary" because he is unworthy to do so will eventually be invited by Hashem to "come into the Sanctuary." The Torah demonstrates to us the importance of modesty and its rewards.

This is a trait that I have always admired about you; you have an unassuming and modest nature, and it is for the most part very pleasant. Having said that, it is important to understand the following observation. Many places in Chazal compare regular bread to haughtiness, since its dough rises, and matzah is compared to modesty, as its dough does not rise. However, even in the matzah there is a little water and potential

---

119 Leviticus 16:2, 3.

to rise. Although we are expected to conduct our lives with humility, at times we have to incorporate a certain assertiveness, especially when it comes to a cause that affects the people around us.

I know it is getting close to the time when you have to consider becoming an officer. Sometimes passivity takes the place of your humility, and that is not always good. If you want to be an officer and it is something you feel would be good for you and your service, then go for it and be aggressive. Make sure that you voice your desires; otherwise you may miss wonderful opportunities to get what you want. Bear this in mind in all decisions for your future, and I think you will find it helpful as you develop and progress.

▶ *I understand what you are saying, and I'm not insulted; quite frankly it comes as no surprise. At the end of the day, it is my service and if I become an officer, I am the one who is making the sacrifice, so this is a decision I have to make myself. I am not sure yet what I want to do.*

I just think sometimes you have to be a "go getter," something that does not come naturally to you. Of course, it's your decision; I just want you to consider all the variables so you can avail yourself of opportunities that may present themselves to you not only now but moving forward.

Acharei Mot

May 1, 2017

▸ *I wanted to share with you something that Rav Eli sent us for Yom Hashoah and Yom Ha'atzmaut.*

Parashat Acharei Mot begins as Hashem instructs Aharon when he can enter the Sanctuary on Yom Kippur. Would it not have been more appropriate for the Torah to give these instructions in Parashat Shemini, immediately after the demise of Aharon's sons Nadav and Avihu? Why wait until now?

The Sanctuary in the Tabernacle and Temple embodied Hashem's Divine Spirit. The Torah did not want Aharon to approach with the fear of death, but rather with reverence and trepidation, because the Sanctuary represented life. It was a place where Aharon came to appeal for the lives of Bnei Yisrael and therefore, while Aharon was expected to approach with fear because of its inherent holiness, he could not approach it with thoughts of death. Therefore, the Torah did not direct Aharon regarding his approach to the Sanctuary right after the loss of his sons, but rather at a time when he could focus on promoting life.

This same principle applies to Yom Hashoah and Yom Ha'atzmaut. Some say the Holocaust was the premise for establishing Medinat Yisrael, but this is wrong because it implies that the impetus for Medinat Yisrael was negative and a consequence of death. Reflecting on the Holocaust is crucial, but it is not the premise for our living here. The Holocaust should instill in us feelings of reflection and rejuvenation, destruction and perpetuation; we do not establish a medinah (country) superficially. The Holocaust should heighten our sense that we live in Eretz Yisrael because of the Divine Spirit it embodies, because it is the essence of holiness and the place where we can get closest to Hashem. Eretz Yisrael and Medinat Yisrael represent our future opportunities to forge a meaningful life.

The Pele Yoetz says that to live in Eretz Yisrael is like experiencing Yom Kippur every day. Eretz Yisrael is the Sanctuary of the Jewish people, and those who live here merit entering the holiest place in the world every single day, as Aharon did when he entered the Sanctuary on Yom Kippur. As we sing in "Hatikvah," "Eretz Tzion virushalayim" (the land of Zion and Yerushalayim) help us stand in awe in the Presence of Hashem.

Kedoshim/Yom Hashoah v'Hagevurah

May 5, 2016

Yakov,

Today is Yom Hashoah (Holocaust Remembrance Day). In Eretz Yisrael, interestingly enough, this day is called Yom Hashoah v'Hagevurah, Holocaust Martyrs' and Heroes' Remembrance Day. Which heroes or act of heroism is the name referring to? The simple understanding is the heroism seen in the Warsaw ghetto uprising, but there is an additional explanation with great significance.

Rav Soloveitchik explained that one reason we perform the mitzvah of counting the Omer[120] immediately following the first day of Pesach is that the exodus from Egypt was all from Hashem, but our future redemption is up to us as well. Therefore, on the second day of Pesach, immediately after we reflect upon Hashem's having taken us out of Egypt, we venture out to the fields, grab the barley with our hands, and thresh it, thereby declaring that redemption is indeed in our hands and, together with Hashem, we facilitate it. I think this is why this day is called Heroes' Remembrance Day, because there is no explanation for the cataclysmic disaster of the Holocaust, but there is a response. While we believe in Hashem and His salvation, we are expected to recognize that we are heroes who responsibly facilitate our future redemption. It is for this reason that Yom Hashoah falls under the days of the calendar which the rabbinate refers to as Yemei Hageulah (Days of Redemption), along with Yom Ha'atzmaut and Yom Yerushalayim.

As a soldier you advance into the field and thresh the barley directly from the ground; you declare that you are willing and able to facilitate

---

120 The Omer is a seven-week period leading up to the maturation of the barley harvest and linking Passover to the Shavuot holiday: at the end of the forty-nine-day counting, we celebrate Shavuot, on which, in the days of the Temple, the first fruits of the crop were brought there as offerings.

our redemption, and you show what it means to join with Hashem in our deliverance. You and your *chevrah* (companions) are the elite responders reminding the world, "Never again."

With love and admiration,

Abba

▶ *Abba, one of the most popular questions posed by my fellow* chayalim *who are secular is if there is a God, then how could He have allowed the Holocaust to happen? I know this is an age-old question, but it is one that cannot be answered, and it is disturbing. It doesn't disturb me as much personally, nor does it shake my foundation of belief in Hashem, but it bothers me that I cannot provide a rational response to my peers. I understand that you too do not have a proper answer or way of explaining, and I appreciate the perspective you shared with me above, but while it is inspiring for me, it does not do the trick for my colleagues.*

It is important to emphasize that the Holocaust is unfortunately not the first catastrophe the Jewish people have experienced. As we proclaim at the Seder, every Jewish generation experiences persecution. But those who believe in God understand that Hashem is infinite, which means that we cannot possibly understand everything He does. We don't have a full perspective on events in this world (tragic and not tragic alike), because we are after all human. I know this response is unsatisfying to a secular person, but it is the best I can do.

Interestingly, survivors of the Holocaust tended to choose one of two paths. They either rejected Hashem because the Holocaust happened or they confirmed their belief in Hashem because the Holocaust happened. I am not comparing or judging at all, but when things become challenging, people classically react by either losing faith completely or by embracing their faith wholeheartedly.

Yom Hazikaron

May 10, 2016

As we find ourselves approaching Yom Hazikaron, there is a very important principle for us to consider. Judaism has always emphasized the importance of remembering. In two weeks' time we will read in the Torah the following *pasuk*: "I will remember My covenant with Jacob and also My covenant with Isaac, and also My covenant with Abraham will I remember, and I will remember the land."[121]

This *pasuk* appears in the middle of Hashem's reprimand to Am Yisrael as He warns them to adhere to the Torah and mitzvot. By reminding us about our forefathers and our connection to Eretz Yisrael, the Torah conveys to us that it is not enough to remember and reflect. Reflection should incite action. On Yom Hazikaron we remember our fallen soldiers and victims of terror, but that should initiate greater responsibility to increase our commitment to Judaism; that is the way to ensure that their martyrdom was not for nothing.

► *Agreed. I think anyone who lives in our country understands at some point or another that this nation cannot exist unless we all make a contribution.*

Correct, and I believe that this is why the main voice of ideology in the army emanates from the Religious Zionist world, because they have the Torah to believe in, which promotes the mitzvah of securing and settling Eretz Yisrael. I will go one step further and offer an observation based on my work with the secular kibbutzim. One of the reasons some of the kibbutznikim are interested in learning about or incorporating some basics of Judaism is not for the sake of observance, but because they seek

---

121 Leviticus 26:42.

the richness of our tradition, if only from a historical and cultural point of view, because they are afraid their children may no longer subscribe to Zionism.

The world is becoming more and more egocentric, and as this happens, the old slogan of the Israeli pioneer who got his hands dirty to till the soil is forgotten. I come across many secular youth and soldiers who are not only disconnected from their Jewish heritage and unacquainted with our forefathers, but they are equally ignorant about the founders of modern Zionism. The same soldiers who don't know who Avraham Avinu was are also unfamiliar with Ze'ev Jabotinsky. As the level of ideology subsides, so goes the level of self-sacrifice and determination. There are pockets of secular Israelis who are aware of this and are genuinely interested in the pioneering ideals. They recognize that the Israeli kibbutznik and pioneer of yesteryear may have believed that his connection to the land via Zionism as opposed to Judaism was enough to ensure Israel's future, but now they see that this is not the case.

▸ *For the large part the secular guys I am with, and you know they are from secular kibbutzim, are very motivated and Zionistic. I don't agree with many of their views, and in fact some of them are so leftist, or at least have been taught to think that way, that to me some of their ideas sound warped. But everything they do and everything they believe in is coming from a good place. They are motivated by ideology and want to give to our country and affiliate with our nation in ways other than religion.*

I am glad to hear that, but I believe strongly that Judaism (not necessarily religion, but in the form of history, culture, and knowledge) has to find its way into their lives, or ultimately their Zionism will suffer as well. This is something we see regularly, as many secular Israelis dodge the draft or opt to leave the country and reside elsewhere, and even intermarry when they are abroad. As Religious Zionists, we believe that Jewish identity and Zionism (and Torah, of course) must go hand in hand to remain intact.

Yom Ha'atzmaut

May 13, 2016

Jeremiah the prophet said, "Blessed is the man who trusts in the Lord; the Lord will be his security."[122]

The *pasuk* establishes a clear partnership between us and Hashem, a partnership that begins with our initiative, as it says: "Blessed is the man who trusts in the Lord." Once we place our trust in Hashem, He will help us believe in Him and "the Lord will be our security." This message resonates as well regarding Eretz Yisrael, which demands our attention and care; we must demonstrate a willingness and desire to invest in it.

May this Yom Ha'atzmaut usher in the redemption of the Jewish people.

▶ *Powerful words, Abba, thank you. I know it is hard for you to be away from Eretz Yisrael and from the family, but you too fulfill a partnership with Hashem by going to the Diaspora and bringing messages and words of inspiration from Israel.*

Happy Yom Ha'atzmaut!

---

122 Jeremiah 17:7.

Emor

May 9, 2016

Parashat Emor begins by delineating all of the laws by which the Kohanim remain holy. Seeing as all of these laws were given to the Kohanim, the Torah did not want Bnei Yisrael to assume that those who were not Kohanim were not holy, which is why immediately following these laws the Torah says: "You shall not profane My holy Name; rather I should be sanctified among the Children of Israel."[123]

This also explains why the laws of all the holidays follow the laws of the Kohanim, because the holidays are the means by which Bnei Yisrael sanctify themselves and the events of the year, as it says: "Speak to the Children of Israel and say to them: The appointed seasons of the Lord, which you shall proclaim to be holy convocations, even these are My appointed seasons."[124]

The Chidushei Harim explains that the holidays are sanctified only because the Jewish people are innately holy. Similarly, as you know, today is Rosh Chodesh. Rosh Chodesh itself is designated by the people; the *beit din* (rabbinical court) in Yerushalayim declares a new month based on people's testimony of seeing the new moon. Once again, the reason we have the power to designate a new month and thereby sanctify the holidays that fall out in that month is because of our inherent holiness.

We are very proud that you got accepted to *course makim* (sergeants' course). Just as the new month arrives, so does a new chapter in your service in Tzahal.

Chodesh tov.

---

123 Leviticus 22:32.
124 Leviticus 23:2.

▶ *Thanks, Abba, but it is really not such a big deal to be accepted to sergeant course; many guys are accepted. I am happy that I have a new challenge coming my way. As you know, it is important to reinvent yourself in the army to avoid the trappings of boredom.*

Everything we accomplish and every new challenge should be recognized and respected; this goes for everything in life. Be proud that you are going into the sergeant course, and welcome it as a fresh opportunity for national commitment and personal growth and development.

Behar

May 23, 2016

▶ *We were supposed to be out for this past Shabbat, and they just told us that because of the situation (the recent attempted terror attacks), we have to stay in; what a bummer.*

You know, it is interesting, because the Torah says that one of the *berachot* we will receive if we follow the decrees of Hashem is "I have broken the bars of your yoke and I led you erect."[125]

Rashi comments, "I led you erect: with an upright stance."

The Maggid of Dubno says that one of the outstanding differences between an animal and a man is that an animal crawls on all fours with its head down, as opposed to a man, who walks with his back straight and head up. Man can stand tall and upright because he can fulfill the decrees of Hashem, which are our source of righteousness and pride.

I know it is not always easy in the army, and it is particularly annoying that you have to be there for Shabbat, but the most important thing is that you are able to hold your head up high "with an upright stance," knowing that you are doing not only the right thing, but a great thing.

---

125 Leviticus 26:13.

Bechukotai

May 29, 2016

Very often we have family discussions on Shabbat regarding why so many youths choose to become nonobservant, and I always remark how difficult it is to understand. I saw something in the *parashah* over Shabbat that I think is significant regarding this issue.

The Torah warns, "If you are revolted by My statutes and if your being is disgusted by My ordinances, so that you will not do all of My commandments, but break My covenant."[126]

Many commentaries explain that rejection of the mitzvot begins when people "are revolted" by the statutes because they don't understand certain mitzvot; when one views mitzvot that are difficult to understand as annoying and burdensome, eventually one will reject the ordinances and mitzvot that one does understand as well. The Torah cannot be fragmented or compromised, and the moment a person starts to embrace those mitzvot that make sense to him and reject those that do not, everything becomes compromised – it's a process known as a "slippery slope."

While I believe there are other causes, I am convinced that what the Torah describes here is the heart of the problem.

▶ Shavua tov *and thanks. Shabbat was actually fine. Your friend Itzik invited me and a number of* chayalim *over for* seudat Shabbat *and I had a chance over Shabbat to go to the Yeshivat Hesder in Hebron for one of the* tefillot.

Phenomenal – he is a good man.

---

126 Leviticus 26:15.

Bamidbar

May 30, 2016

Good morning, Yakov.
The beginning of Sefer Bamidbar confirms that the Torah was given in the desert: "And the Lord spoke to Moses in the desert of Sinai."[127]

There are many explanations regarding why the Torah was given in the desert. The Midrash says, "the Torah is compared to water; just as water cannot rest on a high place and must run downward, so too the Torah can only resonate with someone who places himself like a desert."[128]

Some explain that this midrash refers to modesty. The desert is a bare and desolate place; so too one must view oneself as bare and desolate, always in need of learning more Torah. The desert is also a place that requires nurturing and strenuous effort to make it fertile; so too a person must invest effort to become a *talmid chacham*. Finally, the desert represents loneliness and introspection. A person must decide that he wants to nurture a relationship with Hashem by studying Torah. This applies to Eretz Yisrael as well. Eretz Yisrael is a land that is all about potential. It demands vision and energy, even sacrifice, in order for it to develop and grow. Without sacrifice and desire, it can become a wasteland.

---

127 Numbers 1:1.
128 Midrash, *Numbers Rabbah* 19.

Course Makim – Sergeants' Course

June 1, 2016

Here's a beautiful idea that relates to yesterday's *dvar Torah*. Hashem instructed Moshe to amass an army, saying: "From twenty years old and upward, all that are able, to go forth to war in Israel – you shall count them by their legions."[129]

The simple understanding is that Moshe is told to gather those who are twenty and above to serve in an army. However, the Ramban says that this command is referring to the gathering of the Leviim who are over twenty years of age to serve Hashem in the Mishkan. What prompted the Ramban to veer from the simple context of the directive?

Rav Yakov Ariel explains that the Leviim were naturally fierce warriors. They descended from Levi, who with Shimon had obliterated the city of Shechem. Given their nature, the Leviim would be expected to be drafted into the army, yet they were not. The Torah wanted another important army of soldiers to infuse Am Yisrael with spirituality by serving Hashem in the Mishkan: this would be the job of the Leviim.

Yakov, unfortunately today we do not have a Mishkan or a Mikdash. As a soldier, observant Jew, and as a Levi, you combine your physical service in the army with a spiritual commitment and service as well.

We wish you much success in your sergeants' course.

▶ *Interesting point, and I understand that it is difficult to infuse spirituality into our daily routines. We have reviewed many times how one would expect it to be hard in the framework of the army, but that is not always the case. My friends and I joined Garin Nahal because all*

---

129 Numbers 1:3.

nine of us were interested in demonstrating to our secular colleagues our dedication to Eretz Yisrael, Medinat Yisrael, and Torat Yisrael, serving as a kiddush Hashem. This goal is realized every time we wake up earlier than everyone else to daven in the morning, or each time we avoid certain actions on Shabbat but still fulfill what we are obligated to do. These situations show our friends what we are most committed to and to whom.

Yom Yerushalayim

June 5, 2016

David Hamelech described Yerushalayim, saying: "The built-up Jerusalem is like a city united together."[130]

Yerushalayim is a city that lends itself to unity, which is why the Gemara declares, "Jerusalem cannot be portioned to the tribes [of Israel]"[131]; Yerushalayim belongs to everyone, and every Jew has a portion of it.

Prior to the establishment of Tzahal, the resistance groups Etzel, Lechi, and the Irgun all tried to conquer Yerushalayim, but none were successful. It was not until they merged to form Tzahal that they succeeded, because Yerushalayim demands unity. Unfortunately, the only institution where we find unity today among Am Yisrael is the army, and the only situation when Bnei Yisrael are unified is when there is a war, but that should not be the case. We should learn the importance of uniting peacefully with all of our people and thus merit to witness "the built-up Jerusalem…like a city united together."

Yom Yerushalayim sameach.

▶ *I remember when we used to go together to daven on Yom Yerushalayim in Merkaz Harav Yeshiva; hope we can do it again sometime.* Yom Yerushalayim sameach, *Abba.*

---

130 Psalms 122:3.
131 Babylonian Talmud, *Yoma* 12a.

Egyptian Border: Numbers/ Deuteronomy/Genesis

The majority of service along the Egyptian and Gazan borders consists of patrols. Soldiers maintain consistent shifts surveying the border in jeeps looking out for breaches in the border and attempted infiltration. The average time frame on the border is four to five months.

Bamidbar

May 24, 2017

▸ *Hey, Abba, I am sorry we could not talk for long, considering you are in Australia. I am about to go out on a patrol for a while, so I won't have my phone until around Sunday morning your time. I wanted to explain a little of what's going through my head, so I figured I would text you.*

After finishing course makim *and becoming a* samal *(staff sergeant), on the one hand, I would have liked to continue on for officer training. On the other hand, I've had a lot of thoughts lately about going back to the* mechinah *in November with my friends, to learn and volunteer, which means that either way I could not go for officer training, and maybe it's all for the best.*

I can fight for the officer course, but I'm not one hundred percent sure it's what I want. In the end, if they let me in and then I'm not sure I want it, that's not fair to the army, and it's not fair to someone else who may really want to become an officer. I know that there are positives and negatives either way, and I really need to think about it over the next few days.

I have learned through my experiences in the army, all the way back to when I wasn't able to try out for the Shayetet (elite marine commando unit), that everything happens for a reason and that everything is for the good.

I like the army, and I enjoy protecting our country, but there are many different ways of contributing, and

the army is not the only institution that secures and pro-
tects Am Yisrael.
Love you, have a good week.

You have made me feel very good with what you wrote to me. I am truly impressed with your maturity and sophistication. I was thinking about it a lot over Shabbat and was concerned, but when I turned on my phone on Saturday night and found this message, I was relieved to see the way you deal with things, as I wrote you before Shabbat as well. We are proud of you, and we will be supportive of whatever you decide. You should be very proud of yourself.

Naso

June 8, 2016

A *nazir* (Nazirite) takes a vow to avoid cutting his hair, consuming wine, and other practices as a special devotion to Hashem. When he completes his term (which is at least thirty days), the Torah says that he has to bring a sin offering on the Altar, a sacrifice brought for transgressing a sin. What sin has the *nazir* committed? Shouldn't he be commended for maintaining a spiritual existence?

The Ramban explains that the *nazir* attains spirituality through abstention from wine and meat, from coming in contact with certain people, and from cutting his hair. His entire quest for spirituality is through avoidance of what this world has to offer, and the Ramban says that is not the ideal way to achieve a spiritual life. We are supposed to sanctify Hashem's name in this world by dealing with what is in this world and not avoiding it. We drink wine and eat meat, and by making a *berachah* before doing so; we sanctify an act that would otherwise seem mundane. The *nazir* was unable to sanctify the materials in this world; therefore he had to bring a sin offering.

As an observant *chayal* in Tzahal, you can take combat and physical warfare and translate it into a mitzvah; this seems to be exactly what would be expected from us.

With love and admiration, Abba

▶ *Nice thought, but I respectfully beg to differ on one issue. If serving in Tzahal is a mitzvah in and of itself, then it is not only the observant* chayal *who can do what you described above, but the nonobservant soldier also does it, even though he may not do so intentionally or may not be cognizant of the mitzvah he is fulfilling.*

I agree and stand corrected; thank you for pointing that out. I just want to tell you how sorry I am that you came home and had to go straight back to base the next day because of the terror attack in Tel Aviv. While obviously the attack is most upsetting, I know how difficult that must have been to turn around and go back to base without a break, and I admire your commitment and resilience.

► *It's okay, Abba; you don't have to be sorry. This is exactly what I trained for and, while I wish and pray that these things would never happen, it is times like these when we are able to fulfill what you described above. Isn't this what we are here for? These opportunities prove to be the antithesis of what the nazir did, as we incorporate our physical training into the mitzvah that has been indoctrinated within us for so many years.*

You know, I have to tell you, one of the character traits attributed to Rabbi Akiva by the Gemara is that he would consistently say, "All that happens from the heavens is for the good."[132]

Rabbi Akiva had to deal with many hardships, particularly the Churban Habayit (destruction of the Beit Hamikdash). He was able to somehow derive a positive inspiration from this, in anticipation of the next Beit Hamikdash. This is because he reminded himself that "all that happens from the heavens is for the good."

While your experiences cannot be compared to those of Rabbi Akiva, Mommy and I often discuss how you rarely complain, and you seem to accept difficult situations calmly. That is a great trait to have. Thank you for reminding me of the proper way a person should view life's circumstances. Look after yourself.

---

132 Babylonian Talmud, *Berachot* 60b.

June 1, 2017

Two sons of Levi, Gershon and Merari, were given oxen and wagons donated by the leaders of Am Yisrael, for the sake of carrying various utensils and building materials of the Tabernacle. The only son of Levi who was not given assistance was Kehat, as the Torah says, "But to the sons of Kohath he gave none, because the sacred service belonged to them: they bore them upon their shoulders."[133]

The "sacred service" refers to the Aron Kodesh (Ark) and the Shulchan (Table), which were carried by Kehat personally. These, the holiest of the utensils, had to be carried "upon their shoulders" and not transported by wagons.

The Kotzker Rebbe says that this directive signifies a very important message. One cannot achieve in spirituality without being prepared to "shoulder" the burden and take part in bearing the personal challenges of spiritual development. This really applies to anything in life that is vital and significant. While there is no question as a *chayal* you are obviously part of a collective, as an observant *chayal* you also demonstrate a willingness to take part in this "sacred service" and carry the Aron Kodesh by adhering to the Torah and mitzvot during the course of your service.

---

133 Numbers 7:9.

Behaalotcha

June 9, 2017

In the *haftarah* of Parashat Behaalotcha, the prophet Zechariah says, "…
for behold, I will bring forth My servant the Shoot [Tzemach]."[134]

Zechariah refers to the Messiah as the Shoot or the flourishing one
because his development is similar to that of a tree. At first it does not
appear that the tree is growing; however, with time and patience, if
nurtured with care, the tree's development becomes observable as it
reveals its beauty and produces fruit for others to enjoy.

The same idea applies to the Messiah. The arrival of the Messiah
takes time and patience. We do not recognize or realize who the
Messiah is or how he will reveal himself, yet if we are patient and loyal
to Hashem, then we can play a role in his arrival.

---

134 Zechariah 3:8.

Shelach

June 18, 2017

Parashat Shelach, which we read yesterday, tells about the spies sent by Moshe to assess the land of Canaan for Am Yisrael, and we know that the entire episode was a catastrophe. The *haftarah* of Shelach also informs how Joshua sent two scouts to survey the land of Canaan prior to their conquest, as it says, "Joshua the son of Nun sent out of Shittim two spies secretly, saying, 'Go view the land, and Jericho.'"[135]

The Midrash comments on the meaning of Shittim, "they [the spies] made themselves like clay vessels"; what does this mean?

The Chidushei Harim explains that only the inside of a clay vessel can become impure, but not the outside, because from the outside the clay vessel has no value, and something that is valueless does not become impure. Alternatively, the value of a clay vessel is its capacity to hold things, which is why only the inside of it can become impure.

The scouts Joshua sent "made themselves like clay vessels"; this means they understood that they were external components and unimportant. Rather, it was Hashem's mission to conquer Eretz Yisrael for Am Yisrael that gave them intrinsic value, like the inside of a clay vessel.

A person should never feel prominent because of his stature or identity; he should earn respect based on what he achieves, because that is the source of his value.

This also relates to the reason Parashat Shelach concludes with the mitzvah of tzitzit. The purpose of the tzitzit is to remind us that we can take something in the material realm and elevate it, imbuing it with spiritual purpose. The strings of the tzitzit, which represent the 613 mitzvot, point downward so that looking at them reminds us that through Torah

---

135 Joshua 2:1.

and mitzvot the mundane can be transformed into something profound. One who wears the tzitzit can declare that he knows how to sanctify this world. This is why the mitzvah of tzitzit appears at the end of Parashat Shelach; the spies Moshe sent were incapable of seeing the intrinsic value and holiness of the land of Canaan, and so the *parashah* concludes with the mitzvah of tzitzit.

By the way, while we are on the subject of tzitzit, I noticed that you haven't been wearing them too often. I know that during training and exercises, it is difficult to wear them, and it can be uncomfortable as you sweat up, but what about Shabbat, or can't you just put them on for an hour or so a day? It is an important mitzvah from the Torah, as explained above.

▶ *I don't really wear them often. In the army I wear them only when we are going through a tough exercise or training, when it is most challenging to put them on.*

Why do you wear them then?

▶ *Because I know it is wrong that I don't wear them, so I figure at least I should wear them when it is very difficult and show myself that I have overcome the challenge – kind of like a test to keep myself in the loop of wearing them still.*

Kind of weird, but I kind of get where you are coming from and respect it. I would just encourage you that, as you overcome the challenge, try to wear them a little more consistently. Meanwhile, do the best you can, and it is good that it's on your mind.

Korach

June 27, 2016

Good morning, Yakov. The Mishnah in Avot says: "Every controversy for the sake of Heaven will endure in the end, and every one not for the sake of Heaven will in the end not endure. What was a controversy for the sake of Heaven? Such was the conflict of Hillel and Shammai. And which was not for the sake of Heaven? Such was the conflict of Korah and his entire assemblage."[136]

Why does the Mishnah refer to the conflict that is not for the sake of Heaven as "the conflict of Korah and his entire assemblage," as opposed to calling it the conflict between Korach and Moshe? Korach did not have an issue with his assemblage; he had a dispute with Moshe!

The *Midrash Shmuel* explains that when Moshe confronted Korach, he was serving Hashem, and his intention was "for the sake of Heaven"; but Korach and his assemblage were not interested in Hashem at all, which is why the Mishnah only refers to Korach and his group within the context of a controversy that is "not for the sake of Heaven."

The Noam Elimelech explains that the problems of Korach and his assemblage had nothing to do with Moshe; their issues were among themselves and their need for recognition, leadership, and self-promotion. Moshe was not interested in authority or respect, which is why he is not mentioned in the Mishnah as being involved in a controversy that is "not for the sake of Heaven."

I often warn all of you guys to be very cautious when using the term "for the sake of Heaven," because many murderers claim they do so "for the sake of Heaven," and many thieves claim to pillage "for the sake of Heaven," so one has to use that term carefully, lest what we think is "for the sake of Heaven" and what Hashem defines as "for the sake of

---

136 *Pirkei Avot* 5:17.

Heaven" be two very different meanings. A cause that is "for the sake of Heaven" would appear to be one without any personal agendas.

Baruch Hashem, you are moving into your next stage of leadership, and you are blessed to be immersed in a cause that is visibly "for the sake of Heaven," without any personal interests and strictly for the sake of our nation and people.

June 23, 2017

Good morning, Yakov.
Following the challenge to Moshe and Aharon's leadership by Korach, Hashem instructed Moshe to take the staff of each leader of the twelve tribes, including Aharon, whose name would be inscribed on the staff of Levi, and place them all in the heart of the Mishkan. Moshe was told that the staff of the person who was deserving of leading the nation would flower in the morning as a sign, and the Torah affirms: "And it came to pass the next day, that Moses went into the Tent of the Testimony; and behold, the staff of Aharon of the house of Levi was budded, and put forth buds, and bloomed blossoms, and bore ripe almonds."[137]

Why was it necessary for the Torah to delineate the stages of blossoming on Aharon's staff, as it first says that it put forth buds, then that it bloomed blossoms, and finally that almonds ripened?

Perhaps the Torah is revealing to us the developmental stages of leadership and holiness. One cannot become a successful leader nor attain holiness all at once; it is a process and requires one step at a time. To be a leader for the Jewish people, you first have to sprout buds by studying basics and learning foundations; then you begin to blossom, and finally after much exertion your "almonds" ripen with age and experience.

---

137 Numbers 17:23.

It is important to remember this as well in the framework of leadership in the army and in life in general. To grow into an effective leader, one must invest time and effort; it takes discipline and persistence, but in the end, someone who does so can effectively bear fruit and influence those around him.

B'hatzlachah (good luck) in your new position. We are proud of you.

Chukat

June 25, 2017

Parashat Chukat contains within it the sin Moshe committed by the rock and the punishment he received, as he was denied entry into Eretz Yisrael. Hashem instructed Moshe: "Take the staff, and assemble the congregation, you and Aharon your brother, and speak to the rock before their eyes, that it give forth its water."[138]

It is difficult to understand what Moshe did wrong and why he was punished; many opinions are posed by various commentaries. The Ramban suggests that there were a number of times when Moshe had to cast his staff and strike, for example when he appeared before Pharaoh and turned his staff into a serpent, or when he struck the Reed Sea and it split so that Bnei Yisrael could cross. Here too, when Moshe was told to "take the staff," he assumed that once again he would strike something, and so naturally he was inclined to strike the rock to provide water for the people.

We learn from this Ramban a very important lesson regarding leadership and how to run our lives in general. Even if we are used to certain behaviors or reactions, we should always take a step back and consider that perhaps the present circumstance demands a different reaction than we are accustomed to. Moshe may have been used to using the staff for hitting, but in this particular situation not only was it uncalled for, but it was also wrong.

In every decision we make, we should consider and assess all the variables to make a logical decision, particularly when it comes to issues that affect a nation.

As a *samal* (staff sergeant), you assume a new position of leadership. Obviously, you are expected to lead your soldiers with discipline

---

138 Numbers 20:8.

and to get them into shape, but remember that in all circumstances great leadership demands thorough examination.

▶ *Great stuff, Abba. Thank you.*

June 26, 2017

Boker tov, Yakov.

Yesterday I mentioned the sin of Moshe that appears in this week's *parashah,* where he hits the rock for water rather than speak to it, resulting in Hashem's punishing him by denying him entry to Eretz Yisrael. I also mentioned that there is much discussion among the commentaries as to what exactly Moshe did wrong, but I would like to focus on his reaction to his punishment.

Immediately after Moshe is informed by Hashem that he will not enter Eretz Yisrael "because you did not believe in Me to sanctify Me in the eyes of the Children of Israel,"[139] the Torah does not reveal any reaction by Moshe to his punishment. Moshe led the Jewish people for years in the desert, confronting countless challenges; his one desire to enter Eretz Yisrael was denied, and the Torah tells us: "Moses sent messengers from Kadesh to the king of Edom."[140]

The Torah reveals to us the greatness of Moshe's nature. Although he is denied the one thing that he longs for, and as painful as that might be on a personal level, Moshe does not abandon even for a moment the task at hand. He realizes that he is about to confront the dangerous nation of Edom, sworn enemies of the Jewish people, and that if he does not prepare properly and focus on confronting them, there will be no Jewish nation to speak of. Moshe demonstrates that there is no room for personal calculations when there are national matters to be dealt

---

139 Numbers 20:12.
140 Numbers 20:14.

with; he consistently places the interests of the people and the nation before his personal ones.

This is truly a sign of great leadership.

Baruch Hashem, by putting aside your personal concerns and focusing on the interests of the people and the nation, you have been granted the opportunity to follow in the remarkable footsteps of Moshe Rabbeinu.

▸ *That's a great insight, Abba. To this day I think Tzahal is the only army in the world in which the officers go into battle in front of their soldiers. Hence the famous call which our officers shout to soldiers under their command, "Acharai" (After me), which has become so popularly known regarding Tzahal. We are taught to lead by example for our soldiers and for our nation.*

One of the most difficult issues that *chayalim* had to deal with during Operations Iron Dome and Protective Edge was how Hamas terrorists would shield themselves behind children to avoid being fired upon. In fact, many *chayalim* were traumatized by such scenes, because it is just so foreign to us and disturbing to the extent that even the terrorists know it – which is why they do it – and yet the world continues to insist that we are merciless. It is ironic that Hamas terrorists and hooligans are well aware how compassionate and respectful of life we are, something that the so-called "civilized" world does not recognize about us. We place the interest of people's lives first and foremost, even before our own, as exemplified by Moshe Rabbeinu and by our army to this day. I am proud that this is the army to which you belong and these are the principles to which you subscribe.

Balak

July 10, 2016

When Balak decided to commission Bilaam to curse and thereby undo the Jewish people, he described the Jewish nation as follows: "Behold, a people has come out from Egypt."[141]

Yet when Bilaam repeated his mission to curse the Jewish people, he described them this way: "Behold the people that is coming out of Egypt,"[142] suggesting that the Jewish people are currently coming out of Egypt. Considering that we had already experienced the exodus from Egypt, this usage is inappropriate and grammatically incorrect.

Rav Moshe Feinstein explains that the greatness of Am Yisrael results from the fact that we continuously relive our history; we insist on finding ways to incorporate events of the past into our present-day lives. We are a people who understand that we cannot move forward without first reflecting upon our past. Bilaam was wary of this outstanding feature; he understood exactly where our strength lies and where our resilience comes from, and so he described a people who will always be "coming out of Egypt."

The most effective *chayal* in Tzahal is one who embraces the traditions of our past to ensure our future. A *chayal* who can represent a link between our rich history and our prospective present is a *chayal* who can assure us of a resilient future.

▶ *You often tell a story (and you have written about it) which is presumably true, about a* chayal *who was guarding in one of the army's prisons over Pesach, and he innocently took out a pita bread to eat. One of the terrorist*

---

141 Numbers 22:5.
142 Numbers 22:11.

prisoners reminded the chayal that it was Pesach and prohibited for Jews to eat chametz (leavened grain products), to which the chayal answered that the exodus from Egypt happened thousands of years ago, and the concept of chametz was irrelevant today. The Palestinian responded that if the Jewish people are willing and prepared to compromise their history as something that is "irrelevant today," then the Palestinians are convinced that they can be victorious.

It is unfortunate that so many secular chayalim, many of my comrades, really do not know about and certainly are not connected to our history. I think the problem stems from their lack of education, but also, I feel that if religion were not seen as coercive here in Israel, more secular Jews would be interested in relating to Jewish basics such as the chagim (holidays) and various traditions.

I agree with you one hundred percent. This is exactly the purpose of Makom Meshutaf. We need to get more Jews, particularly secular Israelis, to engage and become interested and connected to our traditions, history, and culture – not only for preservation, but also because there is so much that Judaism has to offer. That is why I really appreciate that you allowed me to speak to your fellow *chayalim* when they came to our house and explain to them the work that we do in the kibbutzim. Particularly Nahal Brigade – as you know, they all come from kibbutzim, and it was a ripe opportunity for me to connect with them and see if I can offer programming in some of their kibbutzim as well. By the way, your friend from Kibbutz Sde Yoav connected me with his dad already, and we are now working on some programming together, so it was beneficial, and I think something will come out of it.

▶ *Oh, wow, that is great, Abba; I did not know. I am glad that is going to work out. Will try to spread the word, but remember I have to be careful - at the end of the day, this is the army, not an educational organization.*

July 11, 2016

Yakov,

Prior to joining the entourage of Moabites to attempt to curse and destroy Am Yisrael, Bilaam speaks with Hashem and Hashem tells him, "If the men come to call you, rise up, go with them; but only the word that I shall speak to you – that shall you do."[143]

It appears that Hashem gives Bilaam the green light to go with the people of Moav; if so, what did Bilaam do wrong?

The Kol Eliyahu explains that Hashem told Bilaam to go, but only with the intent of blessing Bnei Yisrael. Bilaam however went with the messengers of Moav in order to curse Bnei Yisrael, which is why immediately following his departure, the Torah says, "And God's anger was kindled because he went."[144]

Bilaam went with the wrong intentions. This is why the Gemara comments on this *pasuk*, "[From here] we learn that the way a person wants to go is the direction he will ultimately take."[145]

In the end we are responsible for plotting a direction we want to take in our lives, and the question we have to consistently ask ourselves is whether or not we are paving a path toward a positive Jewish life. If we have identified the path we are interested in, then even if we veer off, we can focus on getting back on track.

---

143 Numbers 22:20.
144 Numbers 22:22.
145 Babylonian Talmud, *Makkot* 10b.

July 14, 2016

One of the *berachot* that Bilaam gave to Am Yisrael is "Behold a people that rises up like a lioness and raise itself like a lion."[146]

The Maggid of Dubno explains that the lioness is weaker than the lion. When a person "rises up," he usually does so slowly and with little enthusiasm. However, if he persists, he grows stronger. As he gains momentum and strength, he can "raise [himself] like a lion."

There are great difficulties in life that can affect a person's resolve, but the main thing is to "rise up like a lioness" and begin to move forward, and then one will realize how much he can overcome.

Shlomo Hamelech wrote: "For a righteous person falls seven times, and rises up again."[147] The greatness of a righteous person is not that he never stumbles or makes mistakes. Rather, regardless of the mistakes the righteous inevitably make and the stumbling blocks they encounter, they are not deterred from their aspirations. They "rise like a lioness," and as they proceed, they then "raise [themselves] like a lion."

▶ *Very true. This does not only apply to spiritual progress (although I understand where you are coming from), but also to our physical and tactical training. There are times when the training is difficult and you become discouraged, but much of the resilience and ability to overcome is a frame of mind. If a person convinces himself mentally that he is capable of overcoming, and he commits to the task at hand, he can usually complete it, especially when you look at the big picture and realize that each part of the training brings you one step closer to finishing the course. Thanks.*

---

146 Numbers 23:24.
147 Proverbs 24:16.

Pinchas

July 18, 2016

Good morning, Yakov.

Pinchas's act is referred to as a zealous one, as it says: "Pinchas, son of Elazar, son of Aharon the priest, turned back My wrath from the Children of Israel, in that he was very zealous for My sake among them..."[148]

Generally speaking, acts of zealousness are associated with irrational and radical behavior, yet immediately following this *pasuk*, Hashem says: "Therefore say, Behold, I give him My covenant of peace."[149]

How can "peace" be used in the same context as zealousness?

We can learn from here that fanaticism is rarely acceptable, and the only time it may be permissible is if and when it promotes peace; everything is a question of intentions. Therefore, one must always weigh and measure one's motivations and remember what is appropriate from the Torah's perspective.

▶ *Thanks, but there are many things that remain unclear. How do you define fanaticism? What is radical for one group may be rational for another. I am quite sure that radical Islamists believe that what they are doing is reasonable and will claim that whatever extremism they incorporate is for peace and unity; this might seem warped to us, but to them it is judicious.*

The point you are making is a very good one. I can only provide you with the definition the Torah gives us. Radical Islamists embrace indoctrination

---

148 Numbers 25:11.
149 Numbers 25:12.

and proselytization and claim that those who do not believe in what they do are infidels and deserving of death, as other religions have claimed in the past as well. Not only do we never make that claim, but we also encourage other faiths to keep their belief systems and religions so long as they do not threaten ours and leave us alone. In fact, we discourage people of other faiths from joining ours, and we encourage them to preserve their own; in that sense we are respectful toward other beliefs, even though we do not agree with them.

Pinchas killed Zimri, a Jew, because Zimri deserved the death penalty according to the Torah. Kozbi the Moabite princess was also killed because she threatened the existence of Am Yisrael by enticing the Jewish people to commit forbidden relations; this is obvious. She engaged in sexual relations with Zimri in front of Am Yisrael. Again, we believe that if someone is threatening a Jewish life, we have an obligation to stop that person, even if it means killing him; this is in defense of the Jewish people.

This is also why Tzahal refers to itself as the Israel "Defense" Forces, because, as we have discussed many times, we are not interested in being an aggressor but rather a preserver and protector of Jewish lives, and sometimes that means killing our enemies who threaten the lives of our people. From the Torah's perspective that is not radical, but rather just and righteous.

Sergeant Position

July 20, 2016

Yakov,

Parashat Pinchas contains the one instance in Torah of Moshe using the word *dibbur* to speak to Hashem, as it says: "Moshe spoke [*va'yedaber Moshe*] to the Lord, saying, 'Let the Lord, the God of the spirits of all flesh, set a man over the congregation, who may go out before them, and who may come in before them, and who may lead them out, and who may bring them in.'"[150]

The word *dibbur* (speech) is generally associated with judgment and is a harsh usage of language, particularly when requesting something of Hashem. However, the commentaries explain that Moshe's language was appropriate because it was an expression of concern for appointing a suitable leader for Bnei Yisrael, which was obviously a primary objective.

Moshe describes the nature of a leader by asking for someone "who may go out before them, and who may come in before them, and who may lead them out, and who may bring them in." The Avnei Nezer explains that a good leader is someone who steps in front of the nation for their protection, someone deeply concerned "who may go out before them" without allowing himself to be dragged behind or lost in the crowd. At the same time, a good leader does what is morally sound without allowing the people to influence him or his decisions. This leader "may lead them out [and] bring them in" and guide Am Yisrael accordingly, extending himself for what is correct.

The Chidushei Harim explains that when a leader sees that his people are in a bad place, he "may lead them out" from the impurity and "bring them in" to a pure and better place so that they can try again.

---

150 Numbers 27:15–17.

This *parashah* is read as you complete your sergeant course and become a leader for the soldiers who will be under your command. One of the most difficult aspects of leadership is finding a balance between leading through discipline, knowing when to "lead them out" and distance yourself, and leading with friendship, or knowing when to "bring them in." Remember, to lead a people one first must know how to lead himself. Perhaps this is why Moshe first describes someone who "may go out before them," because one has to work on oneself before working on others. We hope and pray that you will succeed in guiding yourself and your *chayalim* with the proper balance and in the correct direction.

► *I know you often talk about the difficulty as a teacher and even a parent in finding that balance between friend and disciplinarian. I'm afraid that I won't be able to discipline my* chayalim *enough because I'm too laid-back; hope it will be ok.*

There is a famous story of a student of Rabbi Yisrael Salanter who was sent to be the rabbi of a *kehillah* (congregation). Prior to his assuming the position, he went to Rabbi Salanter and told him he was afraid of his new job, to which his rebbe responded, "You want me to send someone who is not afraid?!"

Not only is it okay to be afraid, but that is what is expected and appropriate. There is nothing wrong with learning on the job; this is what life is all about. Learn from and incorporate your experiences, and I am sure you will do fine.

The Gemara lists some of the attributes of the generation of the Messiah, and one of them says, "the face of the generation will be like the face of a dog."[151] Rabbi Yisrael Salanter explains that a dog always appears to lead its master as it walks in front, yet it always looks back to en-

---

151 Babylonian Talmud, *Sotah* 49b.

sure that the master is with him, revealing dependence and uncertainty. The leadership of the generation of the Messiah is the same. Leaders are supposed to believe in themselves and proceed with confidence, but in the generation of the Messiah, the leaders are like dogs; they are always looking over their shoulders, concerned about what people and the press have to say about them. Rather than dictating policy based on what is right, they do so based on public opinion. This demonstrates insecurity and weakness.

A secure person will progress using his attributes and strengths, but he will also consider and accept criticism from others in order to improve.

▶ *Appreciate the advice. On that note, you know I just got my* chayalim, *and as their staff sergeant I have to really discipline them, almost to the point of being mean, which is really not me. I do keep my distance and refrain from any small talk; I only engage with them to give orders. Anyway, I went into the shul and saw one of my chayalim had his shirt out, which is against the rules. I didn't want to bother him during his* tefillah, *so after* tefillah *I pulled him aside and asked him if he ever sees* chayalim *with their shirts out. He told me that he had seen chayalim with their shirts out and he agreed with me that it did not look nice, so I told him that if it does not look right and proper as a* chayal, *certainly when you go in front of Hashem to pray, you should make sure to look respectful.*

You handled that beautifully. Very impressive – I see a future for you as a rabbi.

▶ *I will stick with being a staff sergeant, Abba.*

17 Tammuz

July 24, 2016

Good morning, Yakov.

Today is the seventeenth of Tammuz, a fast day that marks the beginning of the Three Weeks in which we mourn the destruction of the Batei Hamikdash. The Gemara *Sanhedrin* says something strange: "Ben David [the Messiah] will only arrive for a generation that is completely worthy or completely unworthy."[152]

If a generation is completely unworthy, why would the Messiah come, and why is it so important that the generation be "completely" unworthy?

One explanation is that Hashem wants to see how we will react as a nation when the chips are down. When the generation is completely unworthy, that is when everyone must unite and rectify the situation that we find ourselves in. This can only be accomplished when everyone is unified and interested in the same cause, namely improving the predicament of the nation. This unification will rectify the unwarranted hatred that existed amongst Am Yisrael prior to the Churban Habayit and which the Gemara says was one of the causes of the Churban itself.[153]

It is important to note that the Gemara also proposed that the Messiah can come when the generation is "completely worthy," which denotes constructive circumstances. Wouldn't it be wonderful if Am Yisrael could unite under positive conditions rather than negative ones? I sincerely hope that this will materialize someday soon.

---

152 Babylonian Talmud, *Sanhedrin* 98a.
153 Babylonian Talmud, *Yoma* 9b.

Mattot

July 26, 2016

In Parashat Mattot, Moshe instructs Bnei Yisrael, "Extract [and arm] men from among you for the war, that they may go against Midian, to execute the Lord's vengeance on Midian."[154]

The Sefat Emet addresses why the Torah uses the unusual term *hechaltzu*, "extract [and arm]" men, regarding amassing an army. Prior to going to war, a Jew must "extract" any personal interests in order to fully understand that he is fighting for Hashem and for a mitzvah, such as inflicting vengeance on Midian for the Jewish nation and its ideals. This continues to be the case today, not only with the army.

Rashi comments on the text that "men" refers to "righteous men." The Avnei Nezer explains that a righteous person is someone who removes his own concerns to make way for those of a nation and its beliefs. He quotes a Gemara that I often quote, which says: "One who speaks in between donning the phylacteries on his arm and on his head has committed a sin and must return from going out to fight in a war."[155]

The phylactery on the arm represents our physical might, while the phylactery on the head represents our spiritual and intellectual strength. We are expected to connect the two strengths; someone who speaks in between making those two linkages breaks that connection and cannot serve as a soldier in the Jewish army.

Undoubtedly Tzahal has to amass strength for combat and warfare. It needs weapons and tactics in order to remain a physically powerful force. However, as the Jewish army, Tzahal must also represent the phylactery on the head; it must be an army that incorporates ideology, an appreciation of our nation and what its history signifies.

154 Numbers 31:3.
155 Babylonian Talmud, *Sotah* 44b.

▶ *Hey, Abba; really sorry did not respond to your* divrei *Torah but I just read them all. We were out training in the fields for the week and had no access to our cell phones the entire time. This was the hardest week of the army so far. We were out in the cold the entire week, squatting in the thorn bushes, and got pretty ripped up; it was tough and exhausting. I know you like to say that insight about the tefillin on our arm and head. I will attest to the fact that much of the training we did this week required a combination of physical strength as well as mental toughness.*

Gee, Yakov, I'm sorry it was so tough. Believe me, if I could trade places with you, I would.

▶ *Abba, if you could trade places with me, I wouldn't let you.*

July 27, 2016

Yakov,

I offered the following thought to *chayalim* on the border of Gaza during Operation Protective Edge three years ago, in an attempt to en-courage and motivate them, and I wanted to share it with you.

The Torah describes how the people from Shevet Reuven and Shevet Gad approached Moshe and asked permission to settle the Jordan Valley as opposed to Eretz Yisrael: "the land which the Lord smote before the congregation of Israel is a land for cattle, and your servants have cattle."[156]

Moshe does not appear to respond to their request; presumably he was considering bringing their predicament before Hashem. However,

---

156 Numbers 32:4.

the Torah immediately tells us that they asked Moshe again, saying: "If we have found favor in your sight, let this land be given to your servants for a possession; do not bring us over the Jordan."[157]

This time Moshe seems frustrated as he reacts: "Shall your brothers go to the war, while you settle here?"[158]

What spurred Moshe's harsh reaction following the second request as opposed to the first?

After examination, the difference between the two requests becomes clear. The first time Reuven and Gad premised their request to settle the Jordan as a need for their abundant livestock, but the second time they approached Moshe, not only did they ask to settle the land of Jordan but they also added, "do not bring us over the Jordan," revealing that they were not interested in crossing over and settling Eretz Yisrael. This was problematic. Moshe could accept that people may have financial constraints that would obstruct them from living in Israel, as many do to this day, but he still wanted every Jew to know that Eretz Yisrael is the place where he must long to be.

Moshe's reproach, "Shall your brothers go to the war, while you settle here?" was his way of reprimanding Reuven and Gad for revealing that they had little desire to live in Eretz Yisrael, regardless of their practical circumstance.

Tzahal is an institution that helps remind the entire Jewish nation where all of us should long to be, in Eretz Yisrael.

---

157 Numbers 32:5.
158 Numbers 32:6.

Masei

August 1, 2016

When the Torah delineates the laws of the cities of refuge (to which an accidental murderer runs) it says: "and the cities shall be for you for refuge."[159]

The Chidushei Harim says that the words "shall be for you" contain an insightful message for the murderer. While the purpose of the cities of refuge is to provide time for the relatives of the deceased to heal and allow their anger to subside, discouraging them from pursuing the murderer in order to avenge their relation, there is another objective. After all, someone who kills someone else, even accidentally, will feel lost and alone, and so Hashem provides the murderer with a place to collect his senses, gain his composure, and start rebuilding his life.

The Sefat Emet, your great-uncle and the grandson of the Chidushei Harim (your great-great-great uncle), explains that this is precisely the purpose of Sukkot. On Yom Kippur, after revealing and confessing all of our sins, we feel vulnerable and even estranged from Hashem. Hashem provides us with a sukkah, which is essentially a city of refuge, a place we can escape to, away from our homes and our material surroundings. The sukkah is a place where we can introspect, reestablish a rapport with Hashem, and start a constructive life of mitzvot again.

I know that you are stuck in the middle of the desert right now and, while it poses challenges and is not a comfortable situation, you might take this opportunity to see it as a city of refuge, a chance to have some time alone, perhaps an opportune time to reawaken a rapport with Hashem within your private sukkah.

---

159 Numbers 35:12.

Devarim

August 7, 2016

Boker tov, Yakov. Parashat Devarim recounts the journeys and exploits of Bnei Yisrael in the desert. Following their victory over Sichon, the king of the Amorites, and Og, king of the Bashan, the *pasuk* confirms, "But all the cattle, and the spoil of the cities, we took for a bounty for ourselves."[160]

Last week we read in the Torah about how Moshe and Elazar Hakohen instructed Bnei Yisrael to purify the gold that they amassed from the spoils of war during their travels in the desert. In contrast, when Bnei Yisrael would fight to conquer Canaan, they were not allowed to collect any of the booty from the wars, and any riches they acquired were submitted and used for serving Hashem in the Tabernacle. Why were Bnei Yisrael permitted to collect from the wars they fought in the desert, but were not allowed to do so when they fought for Canaan?

Perhaps Hashem wanted Bnei Yisrael to appreciate the intrinsic value of the land of Canaan, Eretz Yisrael. Were Bnei Yisrael to take the riches involved in the conquest of Canaan, it would depreciate the essential greatness and spiritual value of Eretz Yisrael.

One cannot place a price tag on Eretz Yisrael because its spirituality is inherently priceless.

▶ *I remember you telling us a similar thing about the Torah itself. The Torah is referred to as a gift, as it says, "For I have given you a good gift; do not forsake My Torah."[161] You explained that the Torah is the greatest gift because it is valuable not only monetarily but also*

---

160 Deuteronomy 3:7.
161 Proverbs 4:2.

*intrinsically, as well as because it was given by Hashem.
Likewise, Eretz Yisrael as an inheritance from Hashem
to Avraham and the Jewish people, is valuable monetarily and intrinsically by virtue of being a gift from
Hashem.*

Yes, that was an idea I saw in the Chofetz Chayim. There is no doubt that Torah and Eretz Yisrael are naturally bound, which is why the Gemara says, "Rabbi Shimon Bar Yochai said, there are three gifts which Hakadosh Baruch Hu gave to [Am] Yisrael, and all three can only be acquired through sufferings. These are: Torah, Eretz Yisrael, and the World to Come."[162]

Notice how the Gemara says that these gifts can only be acquired through suffering. Usually anything worthwhile takes pain and even sacrifice to secure. Such is the case with Torah and Eretz Yisrael, and that should help explain who you are and why you are doing what you are doing.

August 11, 2016

At the beginning of the *parashah*, Moshe asks Hashem to allow him entry into Eretz Yisrael, saying, "Let me cross over, I pray you, and see the good land that is on the other side of the Jordan."[163]

At first glance the language of the Torah seems superfluous. If Moshe crossed the Jordan, then obviously he would see the land on the other side. I believe the Torah is teaching us a vital lesson. There are people who see Eretz Yisrael but do not necessarily "see the good land"; they find reason to complain and criticize. Moshe says that he wants to "cross over…and see the good land"; he understands the importance of seeing the good of Eretz Yisrael.

---

162 Babylonian Talmud, *Berachot* 5a.
163 Deuteronomy 3:25.

One can choose to be critical and negative about any experience, or one can welcome the opportunities life presents and try to utilize them for constructive purposes. Serving in the army offers many excuses for complaints and disenchantment, but you should try to "see the good land." Mommy is very good at seeing things positively (she is also good at criticizing the fact that I do not). It is nonetheless an important lesson we can all learn from her and an invaluable attribute for us to have in every aspect of our lives.

▶ *Abba, that is a very nice thought, but bear in mind the comparison between the two situations is clearly not justified. During the entire course of his having led the Jewish people through their Exodus and beyond, Moshe longed to arrive in Eretz Yisrael. His vision of Eretz Yisrael was untainted, particularly as it was a fantastic dream embedded in him. Today Eretz Yisrael is a reality, but a very harsh one, as most of us understand that to inherit and secure the Land of Israel we must sacrifice, the most obvious manifestation of which is serving in the army. I appreciate your mentioning Mommy, as it is true, her nature tends to be more optimistic. It is really now, when things are challenging, that one must try one's hardest to gain positive perspective or at least not to become negative, if not from an ideological standpoint, at least from a practical one. Thank you for reminding me of this. It is probably a really difficult thing to remember at all stages of life, as you mentioned.*

Tisha b'Av

August 12, 2016

Yakov,

Tisha b'Av is upon us.[164] Rav Soloveitchik says that part of the reason we cry on Tisha b'Av is that we simply do not miss the Beit Hamikdash and are incapable of appreciating its meaning and value; that in itself is reason to cry.

May we merit understanding the greatness of that which we do not have, and as a result be privileged to see Yerushalayim and its walls rebuilt. Have a meaningful fast.

► *While it is sad that we cannot appreciate the Beit Hamikdash, it is sad to see how many* chayalim *who are with me have absolutely no idea what the Beit Hamikdash was or what it meant to the Jewish people. They also do not know about Tisha b'Av and why we fast. Rav Eli sent us the following text, which I wanted to share with you:*

> *What a privilege we have to live in Eretz Yisrael, a place where even Moshe and Aharon could not enter. Moshe expresses at the beginning of Parashat Vaetchanan: "You have begun to show Your servant Your greatness and Your strong hand, for what god is there in heaven or on earth that can perform according to Your deeds and according to Your mighty acts?"[165]*

---

164 The ninth of Av was Shabbat, August 13; the fast was observed after Shabbat.
165 Deuteronomy 3:24.

Moshe describes what Hashem had "begun to show" him, but we the Jewish people today have been privileged to see and witness the continuation of that beginning. We are privileged to live and dwell in the palace of Hashem; it is hard to imagine.

Yes, I can relate to what you are saying. There are many *chayalim* I speak to who have no idea where Mount Moriah is. They do not know what Har Habayit (the Temple Mount) is or what it once hosted. At least now that your colleagues have come in contact with people like you in the army, they are a bit more familiar with the day of Tisha b'Av and at least aware of something known as the Beit Hamikdash.

Vaetchanan

August 17, 2016

Both last week's and this week's *parashiyot* describe Eretz Yisrael as "a land flowing with milk and honey."[166] Rabbi Motti Greenberg, *rosh yeshivah* of Kerem B'Yavne, explains that the milk in a woman's body is originally blood, as the Gemara says, "blood curdles and becomes milk"[167]; therefore, the milk of a woman, which is pure, originates from blood, which is impure. Honey also originates from a bee, which is impure and not kosher, and it becomes honey, which is kosher and pure. In fact, the Tosafot in *Chullin* discusses why honey is kosher if it originates from a bee, which is not kosher.

The reason Eretz Yisrael is called "a land flowing with milk and honey" is that, just as milk and honey originate from impure sources and require a process to become pure, so too the Land of Israel. Eretz Yisrael is a challenging process; it is a country that needs to develop step by step; but, when it overcomes the obstructions to its existence, it is indeed sweet and pure like milk and honey.

Interestingly enough, the same applies to Israelis. They are also known as a fruit called the sabra. The sabra fruit is prickly and sharp on the outside, but when you open it up, it is soft and sweet on the inside. Israelis appear to be abrasive and rough at first, but after getting acquainted, they reveal that they are actually soft on the inside, kind-hearted and warm people.

▸ *Ha! That's funny.*

---

166 Deuteronomy 6:3, 11:9.
167 Babylonian Talmud, *Niddah* 9a.

Ekev

August 22, 2016

Our *parashah* opens, "And it shall come to pass, because you hearken to these ordinances, and keep and do them, that the Lord your God shall keep with you the covenant and the mercy which He swore to your fathers."[168]

The Torah uses the word *ekev*, which is translated as "hearken," but it also literally means "heel" of the foot. This leads some commentaries to explain that, with every step one takes with his heel, one should hearken and ask himself if he is going in the right direction and walking toward fulfilling the cause of Hashem. If a person knows that every step he takes with his heel is to enhance his relationship with Hashem by fulfilling the ordinances, then he is sure to succeed.

---

168 Deuteronomy 7:12.

Reeh

August 28, 2016

The *parashah* begins, "See, I set before you this day a blessing and a curse."[169]

Some explain this *pasuk* based on the Gemara, which says: A person should always view the world as if it is half worthy and half unworthy [and his actions will tip the world to one direction or the other]. When he does one mitzvah, he influences the entire world toward innocence; when he commits one transgression, he influences the world toward guilt.[170]

This Gemara demonstrates how each one of us can affect the world. For this reason, the Torah uses the singular form in the opening *pasuk* above. Every person is asked to "see" how impactful his individual actions can be, to the extent that he can create "this day a blessing [or] a curse" based on his individual actions. We each have the power to influence and change the world.

With love and admiration,

Abba

August 29, 2016

In the *parashah* there is a very vague directive which says, "You shall not do this to the Lord your God."[171] It is unclear what exactly "this" is that we are not supposed to do. Rashi suggests that it can refer either to the prohibition against offering sacrifices to Hashem wherever one likes, or the prohibition against erasing the name of Hashem. The Kotzker

---

169 Deuteronomy 11:26.
170 Babylonian Talmud, *Kiddushin* 40a.
171 Deuteronomy 12:4.

Rebbe says that the Torah is warning us not to do mitzvot out of habit, merely for the sake of "doing this," without internalizing their purpose and meaning. Performing mitzvot should generate enthusiasm. If our service of Hashem is routine, it will be short-lived and can even lead to exploration of other practices such as idolatry. This is why a *pasuk* prior to this one warns, "You shall utterly destroy all the places where the nations that you are to dispossess served their gods."[172]

Try to be wary of this pitfall and approach your daily mitzvot such as *tefillah* and *berachot* with as much passion as possible. Think back to the enthusiasm you had in the *mechinah*, and perhaps that will help refresh your approach. Most Jews in the world are never given the opportunity to consistently perform the mitzvah of inheriting and settling the land, as you do as a *chayal* in Tzahal.

> ▶ *I appreciate what you are saying, and you're right, the army can become very monotonous. While I understand that our attitude to mitzvot can become a problem in the army, it is just as much a problem when we are not serving in the army. How does one avoid these traps as a civilian? How does one avoid getting bored by the same* tefillah *or keep from getting fed up from wearing tzitzit? Perhaps right now this problem is prevalent in the army, but it is a consistent challenge for any Jew under regular circumstances outside the framework of the army as well.*

You are one hundred percent correct, and that is precisely why the Midrash comments on the *pasuk* which I related to you yesterday: "'See, I set before you this day a blessing and a curse' – Why does it say 'this day'? Because every single day, one should view the mitzvot as if they were given anew."[173]

---

172 Deuteronomy 12:2.
173 Midrash, *Lekach Tov*, Nitzavim 52a.

Chazal knew this was a difficult challenge to deal with. Refreshing our attitude and approach to the mitzvot requires devotion and innovation every day. Part of the answer is finding ways to enhance involvement; for example, leading the services as you get older and learning in groups that allow you to express your own ideas and arguments. These opportunities help you feel that you are a meaningful part of the picture. In addition, the more you learn and study, the deeper your understanding of the mitzvot, which strengthens your commitment to performing them as well. With sophistication comes dedication.

August 30, 2016

In the middle of warning against following a false prophet, the Torah instructs, "After the Lord your God shall you walk, and Him shall you fear, and His commandments shall you keep, and to His voice shall you hearken, and Him shall you serve, and to Him shall you cleave."[174]

One of the questions posed regarding this *pasuk* is that virtually the same words appear in Parashat Ekev prior to this one, as it says, "You shall fear the Lord your God, Him shall you serve, and to Him shall you cleave."[175]

What is the difference between the two verses?

The Chidushei Harim explains based on the context of each *pasuk* and whom each directive is addressing. The first *pasuk* in Ekev addresses the individual and instructs him to fear, serve, and even cling to God. However, the directive in Reeh addresses the nation, which is why its usage is plural; it is warning the entire Jewish people regarding false prophecy, because in order to avoid the trap of a false prophet, it is necessary to have collective strength.

What we learn from here is that while a person is required to grow and develop as an individual, that is not always sufficient. At times a

174 Deuteronomy 13:5.
175 Deuteronomy 10:20.

group effort is required to stimulate or preserve positive growth and development. This helps explain the importance of *tefillah* with a minyan, or the ability to annul one's vows only in front of a group that constitutes a court, or even the importance of learning with a *chavruta* (study partner). A united group effort should not be underestimated, as I am sure you in the army know better than anyone. Serving in the army is also based upon recognizing the strength of a collective. Particularly in your case, where the nine of you became *chayalim* as a *garin*, you did so because all of you understood that there would be challenges both physical and spiritual, and you all realized the advantage of uniting. It is through this effort as representatives of a nation that you will succeed in following Hashem, fearing Hashem, observing His commandments, and cleaving to Him.

August 31, 2016

Good morning, Yakov.

Hashem promised Bnei Yisrael after they crossed the Jordan, "But when you go over the Jordan, and dwell in the land that the Lord your God, causes you to inherit, and He gives you rest from all your enemies all around, so that you will dwell securely."[176]

The text is repetitive; if Hashem "gives you rest from all your enemies," then surely "you will dwell securely"?

Rabbi Yehonatan Eybeshitz explains that the first part of the verse, "rest from all your enemies," refers to the blatant enemies from surrounding nations, and the threats from foreign countries. However, the second part of the verse, "you will dwell securely," refers to peace and unity from within; there will be unity among the Jewish people themselves, which, at times, is far more challenging to achieve. In fact, Rabbi Eybeshitz explains that this second part of the verse is conditional; when

---

176 Deuteronomy 12:10.

the Jewish people "dwell securely" with one another, then Hashem will assure that they will "rest from all their enemies."

This understanding of Rabbi Eybeshitz is quite appropriate, as Rashi explains that the context of the verse denotes that, after conquering the Jordan and Israel, the land would be divided among the twelve tribes of Israel. Often inheritances and land portions can be divisive, even among close relatives. The Torah assures us that when Eretz Yisrael is divided proportionately, everyone will accept his portion and respect each tribe's territory.

Shabbat shalom.

▶ *Thank you for coming by today and bringing such nice food for Shabbat. We will all enjoy; the guys love Mommy's challah. Everyone has their own way of connecting, which is nice. Shabbat shalom and love to all.*

Shoftim

September 7, 2016

Good morning, Yakov.

This *parashah* includes the halachah that a king has to write a *sefer Torah*, as it says: "he shall write for himself two copies of this Torah in a book.... And it shall be with him, and he shall read therein all the days of his life, that he may learn to fear the Lord his God."[177]

If the Torah is "with him," was it necessary to instruct that the king "shall read therein all the days of his life"? It seems obvious that is what the king will do with his personal Torah!

The Meshech Chochmah explains that the seemingly redundant language highlights the importance of the law in the Talmud that states, "Teachings which are [part of] the written law are not allowed to be recited orally."[178]

One is obligated to read the text of the written word as opposed to reciting it by rote. Therefore, the king is instructed to "read therein" from the text of the Torah that is with him, not to recite it orally, and in this way the rest of the Jewish people are also reminded of this law, which applies to them as well.

The Chatam Sofer says that the Torah is warning someone of stature, such as a king or a leader of Am Yisrael, who may tend to think highly of himself, that it is not sufficient that the Torah "shall be with him." The king is expected to "read therein all the days of his life"; he must seek guidance and wisdom from scholars in order to consistently appreciate and subscribe to the Torah even more.

Perhaps this is what the Torah wants to teach all of us. It is not enough that the Torah be "with you"; one must "read therein all the

---

177 Deuteronomy 17:18–19.
178 Babylonian Talmud, *Gittin* 60b.

186 | Armed with Spirit

days of his life" in order to incorporate its wisdom and ideals incessantly. The depths of the Torah are truly amazing, and the more we "read therein," the more we value its profundity. This is why I remind you that whenever you have a little time, even if it is just a few minutes, take out a *sefer* and "read therein"; you will be amazed how enlightening and beneficial even those few minutes can be.

▶ *The hardest part of what you are suggesting is not the interval of time, because it makes no difference if it is for an hour or just for ten minutes; the difficulty is bringing myself to take out the* sefer. *I am tired, and when I have a few minutes I want to use the time to sleep or to chill. I appreciate the value of your words, but I am not sure how to use them practically.*

Everything constructive requires sacrifice in some form or fashion; you as a *chayal* know that to be true, more than many other people, but one does not and is not expected to construct an entire city in one day. Take small steps toward making that sacrifice. If allocating ten minutes a day to learn something is too challenging at this point, then take two minutes (which is one of the points of my sending you these *divrei Torah* every day). Those two minutes are also difficult to commit to, but they represent a step to build upon, much like training for a marathon. Perhaps take the two minutes of learning right after you daven any one of the *tefillot*; this way you are already in a spiritually motivated frame of mind.

September 9, 2016

Boker tov, Yakov.

With regard to *eidim zomemim* (conspiring witnesses), the Torah says, "You shall do to him as he had conspired to do to his brother."[179]

The Mishnah comments on this *pasuk*, "Conspiring witnesses are not executed unless the verdict [condemning the accused] has been pronounced, for the Sadducees maintained [that the conspiring witnesses are not executed] unless [the accused] has been put to death, as it says, 'life for life.' The Sages replied to them, but is it not stated earlier [regarding conspiring witnesses], 'and you shall do to him as he had conspired to do to his brother [and not as he succeeded in doing to his brother],' and so his brother must be still alive." And the Talmud adds, "If the conspiring witnesses have not yet killed their victim [the accused], they are executed [for their false testimony]; however, if they killed the accused [as a result of the conspiring witnesses' testimony], the conspiring witnesses are not executed."[180]

The premise for the Sages in the Mishnah to refute the interpretation of the Sadducees is that the word *brother* refers to someone who is still alive, and so if the accused is alive, he falls into the category of a "brother," and only then do we execute the conspiring witnesses as a punishment. The Ritba points out that there are many times in the context of the Torah when the word *brother* is also used regarding a deceased person. For example, in the case of a levirate marriage, when someone performs the mitzvah of marrying his late brother's wife to establish a family in his name, the Torah says, "It shall be that the first-born that she bears shall succeed in the name of his dead brother…"[181] The premise of the Sages in the Mishnah would therefore seem to be refuted, and it would appear that the Sadducees are correct.

---

179 Deuteronomy 19:19.
180 Babylonian Talmud, *Makkot* 5b.
181 Deuteronomy 25:6.

188 | *Armed with Spirit*

The Ritba offers a profound insight and explains that, when referring to a brother from the same family and the same relation, then the term *brother* is used in the Torah even for a brother who is dead, which is why in the case of a levirate marriage *brother* is used. Otherwise, *brother* is only used in the context of performing mitzvot, in which case the term is not relevant to a deceased because he can no longer perform mitzvot. Hence, the opinion of the Sages now makes sense because it says, "You shall do to him as he had conspired to do to his brother"; so long as the accused is alive, he is called a "brother" in terms of his ability to perform mitzvot and so the conspiring witnesses are put to death as punishment, but once the accused is dead, he is no longer considered a "brother," and the law of "you shall do to him as he conspired" no longer applies.

The only time Jewish people can refer to themselves as "brothers" is when they help one another and perform mitzvot. Appropriately, the term *brother* is used daily in the context of the army, which makes perfect sense because all *chayalim*, regardless of their affiliation, are inevitably bound like brothers by the mitzvah of securing, settling, and inheriting Eretz Yisrael. We should be blessed to always call ourselves "brothers" as a result of a common interest.

On a similar note, at the end of the *parashah*, Am Yisrael are instructed in preparation for war, "When you go forth to battle against your enemy.... [The priest] shall say to them, 'Hear, O Israel, you are coming near this day to the battle against your enemies.'"[182]

The word *hear* is often used in the Torah as a means of emphasizing gathering, as it says: "And Moses and the priests the Levites spoke to all Israel, saying, 'Keep silence and hear, O Israel: This day you have become a people to the Lord your God.'"[183]

If follows that here in our *parashah*, the Torah is directing Am Yisrael prior to going out to war. "Hear. O Israel," as a unification, is a prerequisite to victory.

---

182 Deuteronomy 20:1, 3.
183 Deuteronomy 27:9.

May you and your brothers in arms respect one another, listen to and hear one another, and, as a result of your efforts to unite, we should be privileged to experience the words of this week's *haftarah*, "It is I; I am He Who comforts you."[184]

▶ *Tzahal unites us through combat. Don't get me wrong; there are nice things that emerge from togetherness in the army, such as the ability to demonstrate some mitzvot to my secular peers, or even the dialogue we engage in at times, but the point of your* dvar Torah *above is that we have to feel like brothers in times of peace, outside a framework of challenges such as the army. I am friendly with secular guys in my unit, but I am not sure what the future will bring or whether we will remain friends as civilians, because everyone will go his own way, and those ways are distinct to a secular and an observant person. I hope I am wrong.*

What you say is true. At the very best you will each learn from each other, respect one another as I am sure you do already, and continue a rapport that can serve as an example to others outside the framework of Tzahal. At worst, each of you will have at least become aware of your differences and that you were willing to put them aside, and maybe that concept will resonate in your civilian lives as well. Case in point: as a result of your friendship with "Schmooze" in the army, I have been in touch with his father on their secular kibbutz, Sde Yoav, and he wants to facilitate my visiting the kibbutz to do a program on basics of Judaism, so never underestimate the impact this unification has outside the army as well.

---

184 Isaiah 51:12.

Ki Tetzei

September 11, 2016

Parashat Ki Tetzei opens, "When you [singular] go forth to battle against your enemies, and the Lord your God delivers them him into your hands."[185]

This use of the singular form prompts many commentaries to explain that the *pasuk* is not only speaking about a war of national concerns, but also our personal wars, such as our need to wage war against the evil inclination, as the Talmud says, "Rabbi Shimon Ben Lakish says that a man's inclination overcomes him every day and seeks to kill him, as it says: 'The wicked one watches for the righteous and seeks to kill him.'"[186]

It is important to recognize that overcoming the evil inclination is indeed a battle that sometimes requires waging war, but if a person takes preliminary steps to do so then Hashem will deliver it into your hand.

This same idea appears in the Talmud, which states, "One who attempts to purify himself will receive assistance to become pure."[187]

Purity and sanctity emerge only when we allow them to, by beginning the process and making promises to Hashem, but one has to at least show he wants to change. This is precisely what the month of Elul is about; we have to decide to head in a different direction as we approach Rosh Hashanah and Yom Kippur.

---

185 Deuteronomy 21:10.
186 Babylonian Talmud, *Sukkah* 52b.
187 Babylonian Talmud, *Shabbat* 104a.

September 12, 2016

Good morning, Yakov.

Regarding a *ben sorer u'moreh* (rebellious son), the parents have to declare that he "does not listen to our voice..."[188]

The Mishnah establishes, based on this excerpt from the *pasuk*, that if one of the parents is deaf, then the child can never be considered a rebellious son;[189] the question is why not? After all, it is the son who doesn't listen to his parents, and that has nothing to do with the parent's ability to hear.

Rav Shimshon Raphael Hirsch explains that this law reveals a remarkably important lesson regarding successful parenting. One of the most important attributes for parents to have is the ability to listen and be attentive, not only to their children's needs but also to the expectations they have of their children. If parents demand things of their children but do not follow those same demands themselves, then they are not listening either; this hypocrisy can be noticeably detrimental to a child's development. Rav Hirsch says that when the parents state that their son "does not listen" to them, they are also announcing their failure to listen to their child's needs, which is why the Mishnah determines that a deaf parent – physically and symbolically one who is not attentive to his son's needs – cannot have a rebellious son, since the parent is largely responsible for causing the son to rebel.

The message of Rav Hirsch rings loud and clear. We often discuss children who choose different lifestyles from their parents, or who rebel against religious observance (the term we use today, "off the derech," originates from this rebellious son in the Torah, who is described as being "wayward"), and why or where their opposition originates from. One thing that seems certain is that if a parent (or I guess anyone in

---

188 Deuteronomy 21:20.
189 Babylonian Talmud, *Sanhedrin* 71a.

a relationship, for that matter) does not listen to his or her child, the chances are greater that the child will grow disenchanted with what the parent would like to offer.

It's funny, because life in the army is all about giving and following orders, but real life outside the army is not about orders at all; people don't respond to orders. It is about listening to others and learning from others' experiences. I have always felt that you are a pretty good listener (certainly a better listener than talker), which should help you create successful relationships.

▶ *I get what you are saying. I know that I am not a big conversationalist, but that doesn't mean I am always listening or willing to listen. Sorry that sometimes when you talk to me I am a bit abrasive; when I am home many times I just don't really feel like talking, especially not about heavy stuff like religious direction.*

The hard part about being a parent is that you have to listen, but if you are only listening and not guiding or directing, then there is a problem. That is why I feel it is my obligation to talk as well and to throw reminders, suggestions, and even requests your way regarding life and the decisions you make. I suppose each of us has to work on incorporating this balance of listening and conversing accordingly. It's good that we can express this openly.

September 12, 2016

Yakov,

I thought I would share with you the following reflection based on our exchange earlier today.

Why do so many of our youth who consider themselves observant reject many *mitzvot d'rabbanan* (rabbinic mitzvot)? There are a number of ways I am familiar with (and you might be as well) in which this trend reveals itself.

Many young men who are observant no longer wear kippot, or they will casually remove them at various times during the course of the day. I recently engaged in conversation with a number of observant young couples who informed me that some of the wives keep seven days before going to the mikvah, which are binding from the Torah, but they do not count the five extra days tacked on as a rabbinic decree since the time of the Talmud to help avoid confusion and maintain the institution of purity. Many young people casually touch each other, either putting their arms around each other in a friendly manner, or even greeting one another with gestures of affection such as a hug or kiss. Some young couples have told me that it is "custom" among many of their friends for one's wife to sit on the lap of someone else's spouse. These halachic wrongdoings are predominantly rabbinic prohibitions (although according to some commentaries they fall into transgressions from the Torah) and they beg the question: Where is the rejection of rabbinic directives and guidelines coming from?

Just last week we read in the Torah, "...you shall not deviate from the sentence that they [rabbinic leadership] will tell you, to the right, nor to the left."[190]

There are only two mitzvot in the Torah that ensure if you keep them "it will be good for you and will prolong your days"; the mitzvah of respecting one's parents[191] and the mitzvah of *shiluach haken* – sending the mother bird away prior to taking its eggs, which appears in this week's *parashah*.[192] The Talmud explains that the mitzvah of *shiluach haken* is what one would consider an "easier" mitzvah because it does not incur financial disbursement, while the mitzvah of respecting one's parents is more challenging, since it can incur monetary commitments.

---

190 Deuteronomy 17:11.
191 Deuteronomy 5:15.
192 Deuteronomy 22:6–7.

The Torah joins the two by delineating the reward one receives when fulfilling either one because, as Rashi explains, we are meant to approach all mitzvot with the same urgency, as the Mishnah in *Avot* says, "Be as careful and cautious with a minor mitzvah as with a weighty one."[193]

Perhaps if you are home this Shabbat, we can discuss a bit more why many of our youngsters do not necessarily subscribe to the approach clearly laid out in this past week's *parashah*. Meanwhile, I leave it with you as food for thought.

September 13, 2016

Good morning, Yakov.

One who fulfills the mitzvah of *shiluach haken* (sending the mother bird from the nest prior to taking its eggs) is rewarded, "so that it will be good for you and will prolong your days."[194]

Immediately following, the Torah instructs regarding another mitzvah: "When you build a new house, you shall make a fence for your roof, that you not bring blood upon your house, if any man fall from it."[195]

The Binyan Ariel explains that a person who is assured by Hashem that his days will be prolonged may have no concerns regarding his own safety, but he must continue to show concern for the safety of the people around him. This is why, immediately after revealing the reward for fulfilling the mitzvah of *shiluach haken*, the Torah demands from that same person to "make a fence for your roof" to ensure that no one else should "fall from it."

A Jew must always demonstrate concern for the safety of others, even if he is comfortable. Mommy and I have fulfilled the mitzvah of *shiluach haken* by sending you off from our nest and home to serve in the

---

193 *Pirkei Avot* 2:1.
194 Deuteronomy 22:7.
195 Deuteronomy 22:8.

army, and, now you fulfill the mitzvah of making a fence to secure our people. Hashem should prolong your days as well.

▶ *Thanks very much, Abba, but the difference is that one is granted the reward of prolonged days because he fulfills a mitzvah he is not obligated to do and goes beyond the call of duty. Serving in the army is not by choice; we are required to do so. While I appreciate your admiration, I am not sure it is well deserved or comparable in this instance.*

From a halachic perspective you are right, the reward is for fulfilling a mitzvah that is beyond the call of duty, and so there is no comparison. However, there are plenty of people who are able but choose not to serve in the army; they flee from their obligations, which you do not. There are many who serve in the army half-heartedly and they would prefer to be elsewhere, but you serve with a positive attitude and with the aspiration to fulfill a *kiddush Hashem* through your service. For these reasons you deserve to be commended and perhaps rewarded by Hashem.

▶ *You know the Mishnah that says, "Do not be like servants who serve their master for the sake of receiving a reward, but be rather like servants who serve their master without the express intention of receiving a reward; and let the fear of Heaven be upon you."[196]*
I am not serving in the army to receive reward or score points, I am doing it because it is an obligation to do so. I consider it rewarding and a privilege to serve in and of itself.

---

196 *Pirkei Avot* 1:3.

Ki Tavo

September 22, 2016

▶ *Abba, one of the* berachot *that the Torah confirms Am Yisrael will receive if they follow the mitzvot is "Blessed shall you be in the city, and blessed shall you be in the field."*[197]

There are people who fulfill mitzvot in the comfort of their own homes, yet the moment they leave their familiar surroundings and find themselves outside the confines of their homes, they no longer adhere to the mitzvot because their commitment was not strong enough to begin with. I imagine this is why Hashem offers a berachah *both for "in the city" and our comfort zone of adherence, as well as "in the field," which is away from our normal surroundings where it is more challenging to keep the mitzvot.*

There is no question that it is much harder to follow the Torah when you are "in the field," as I and many other chayalim *have experienced in the army. I know guys who have had problems on smaller bases with the ovens, because nonobservant* chayalim *will make the meaty oven non-kosher. Late at night they innocently make a grilled cheese sandwich in the meaty oven (even though you and I know that violating* kashrut *regulations is also against army law). They don't do this intentionally, but they don't keep kosher, and so they are not familiar with* kashrut *restrictions. I called you once a little while*

---

back because someone's father, who was secular, brought food to the base, and I was not sure where it came from. Believe me, when the whole group is eating fresh food and enjoying it, you begin to justify why it is probably okay to eat with the guys. It is challenging to refrain from partaking with them or at least thinking about it.

We just finished a twenty-kilometer trek through the night, and when our officers finally gave us some time to rest, it was already past sunrise and time for Shacharit, so while everyone rested and slept a bit, I had to take precious resting time to put on tefillin and daven. I know these things sound elementary, and it may be obvious to you or others that one would still keep the mitzvot under such circumstances, but it is not so. It becomes very demanding and sometimes frustrating to adhere to observance on a proper level. These are some of the things we have to go through, and it explains the cliché that many observant soldiers grow weaker in their observance while in the army. This is exactly why the mechinah promised us they would visit us periodically and offer us shiurim (classes) during our service (which unfortunately, as you know, they have not lived up to), and this is why many yeshivas and mechinot have a "roaming rabbi" or rabbis who come around to offer shiurim to their students. I heard that unfortunately this venture does not pan out as much as expected either. Nonetheless, I am aware of the variables and try to push myself to stay committed as much as possible. The divrei Torah you send daily help provide me with a little shot in the arm. Thanks.

Listen, many of the challenges you relate above are very common within the framework of the army. In fact, your brother-in-law, Yakov Chaim, when he was chief on the Dabur patrol boat in the navy told me that he had to constantly deal with *kashrut* issues and that many times, when his crew would go out to eat, he was unable to attend. This was disconcerting for him, but he is a solid guy and a *ben Torah* committed to mitzvot. The reason I mention this is that it's important for you to recognize that many have successfully dealt with these issues and have remained strong and steadfast in their faith and observance; you are not alone, and you can certainly do so as well.

▶ *I will try my best.*

That is all anyone can expect. Love you, buddy.

Nitzavim

September 25, 2016

"You are standing this day all of you before the Lord your God: the heads of your tribes, your elders, and your officers – all the men of Israel."[198]

Normally Moshe addresses the leaders of Israel first, but here the *pasuk* emphasizes that he addressed "all the men of Israel." The Alshich points out that when it comes to standing before Hashem, it does not matter whether you are "heads of your tribes, elders, [or] ...officers." "All the men of Israel" have equal opportunity to create a rapport with Hashem, and only He knows who is actually closer to Him.

Thanks for joining us for the Machane Meshutaf Shabbat; it was nice to be all together.

▶ *It was a great Shabbat. I wanted you to know that I admire you a lot. I could see over the Shabbat of Machane Meshutaf how much people respect you and how everyone knows who you are. It is impressive that they chose you to speak out of over two hundred lecturers, and even where they place you to sit means that they respect you. I also enjoyed learning that you can lecture to all types in various situations, which is not easy to do; all this says a lot about the hard work you do.*

It's a real blessing not only to enjoy your work, but to also know that your work can inspire others, particularly *chayalim*. Baruch Hashem, I have the privilege to feel this way, and thank you for recognizing it and sharing it with me.

---

198 Deuteronomy 29:9.

September 29, 2016

▶ *It is a sad day today with the passing of Shimon Peres. Although we disagreed with a lot of things he said, the country today would really not exist without him. The fact that many people strongly disagreed with his ideas also shows that his opinion was important to people, and for good reason. He gave and sacrificed a lot because he only wanted the good of the country. He was an amazing person of influence, which you can see just by all the people who came to his funeral. He built the nuclear plant in Dimona and developed the high-tech industry here; Israel is a great country because of him.*

I have to say we just don't have pioneers like him around anymore, people who just sacrificed for our country. Although I disagreed with a lot of his policies (and even got angry regarding many of them), I don't think there is any question that his intentions were in the right place.

September 15, 2017

Nitzavim reminds the Jewish people to remain committed and loyal to our covenant with Hashem. There is reference in the *parashah* to the concept of *teshuvah* (repentance), and in fact the Ramban derives that there is a mitzvah of *teshuvah* from these same *pesukim*. In the heart of this discourse, Moshe tells Bnei Yisrael in the name of Hashem, "Then the Lord your God will bring back your captivity and have compassion on you, and will return and gather you in from all the peoples to which the Lord your God has scattered you."[199]

---

199 Deuteronomy 30:3.

Why is it necessary to say that Hashem will bring us back from captivity and that He will gather us in from where we were scattered? Are these two statements not one and the same?

The Meshech Chochmah explains that the first statement, that Hashem "will bring back your captivity," refers to those Jewish people who have always longed to be in Eretz Yisrael and have taken measures and made sacrifices to do so. This is precisely why Hashem says that He "will have compassion on [them]." However, some of the Jewish people do not yearn to be in Israel and have grown comfortable remaining in the Diaspora. To these people, Hashem vows that He "will return and gather [them] in from all the peoples," foreign nations and strange lands where they are scattered, and they too will dwell in Eretz Yisrael.

Vayelech

September 17, 2017

Good afternoon, Yakov.

Every year when Parashat Vayelech comes around, I think about a sad but insightful comment which Rav Moshe Feinstein explains. The *parashah* describes Moshe's departure from the Jewish people and begins by stating, "Moshe went…"[200]

Rav Moshe notes that this usage describes the fact that regardless of Moshe's greatness, in the end he was unable to fulfill the mission of bringing Am Yisrael into Eretz Yisrael.[201] It was as if "Moshe went" prior to completing his mission and left Bnei Yisrael mid-process.

In life it is important to set goals, but then the next most important thing to do is to try to complete them. Food for thought for all of us.

▶ *I have heard this from you before, and it is a really nice lesson. Thank you. Interestingly enough, the army is a place that lends itself to setting goals, from waking up in the morning on time to completing a guard rotation to finalizing a mission, as you know. I know that you are referring to long-term goals, but I am not ready for that yet. In the army I just have to take one step at a time. When I am finished, im yirtzeh Hashem (God willing), then I can start focusing on longer term goals, and I not only hope they will be good ones, but I hope and pray they will come to fruition. Bear in mind, Abba, that this is of course after my post-army trip and excursion somewhere out of Israel. ☺*

---

200 Deuteronomy 31:1.
201 Rav Moshe Feinstein, *Darash Moshe* 166.

Haazinu

September 20, 2017

Good morning, Yakov.

One of the wishes that Moshe expresses as he offers his *berachot* to Bnei Yisrael in the song that he sings in Parashat Haazinu is "My doctrine shall drop as the rain, my speech shall distil as the dew."[202]

Rabbi Simcha Bunim of Peshischa explains that Moshe connects teaching to drops of rain because when it rains, one does not see the immediate effects of the droplets. Only after a period of time can one appreciate the effect that the rain had on the ground and reap the benefits of the produce nurtured by the rain. So too with regard to learning Torah. One does not always see the benefits of the teaching of the Torah, and of life for that matter, immediately. Sometimes one appreciates the teachings and foundations that he received from learning Torah only over a period of time, and it is then that one recognizes the depth and greatness of what the Torah has to offer during the course of one's lifetime.

This is such a vital lesson because when one views every experience (particularly the very challenging and difficult ones such as those that you encounter in the army) as a learning opportunity, all of a sudden the challenges become more manageable and at times perhaps even welcome.

I think this is a productive way to approach our new year which we have just begun and certainly for you to approach all the new and challenging encounters you will inevitably have to deal with during your time as a *chayal*.

---

202 Deuteronomy 32:2.

▶ *Very true, Abba. There are many basic foundations that one can take for granted being reared in an observant home and sent to yeshivot my whole life, from putting on a kippah first thing in the morning to davening every day and putting on tefillin. All of a sudden as a* chayal, *the focus becomes how to be a soldier, and sometimes being observant becomes secondary. As a result, putting on tefillin, davening every day, and trying to set aside some time to learn something is no longer automatic. I suppose that were it not for those "drops of rain," the teachings and foundations that you and Mommy provided me with, it would be even more challenging to adhere to them.*

Thank you, Yakov. You will find with time, God willing, that nothing in life should be taken for granted, particularly the determination and investment it takes to be committed, not only to the Torah, but to anything valuable and sacred in your life. If you continue to appreciate this, then indeed the "drops of rain" will have been worth all our efforts.

Yom Kippur

October 9, 2016

After a person brings a sin offering, the Torah instructs regarding the utensil it was brought in: "But the earthenware vessel in which it was cooked shall be broken."[203]

Why is one required to break the earthenware vessel that a sin offering was cooked in?

The Kli Yakar explains that earthenware is extremely absorbent, which is why the only way to purify it is by breaking it, and the same with regard to someone who has sinned. A person (known in Hebrew as *adam*, from the word *adamah*, which means earth) who sins absorbs the effects of the sin, and the only way for him to purge himself is by experiencing remorse and expressing regret, to the extent that he feels broken; only then is he purified, just like an earthenware vessel that is broken. One can only construct a new rapport with Hashem after first understanding the need to do so.

We all sin and make mistakes, but so long as we feel remorse and pain for what we did, showing a desire to do otherwise, we can begin again.

Gmar chatimah tovah (may you be sealed in the Book of Life).

With love and admiration,

Abba

▶ *Thank you very much, Abba, for all that you have done and continue to do for me. If I said or did anything to offend or hurt you, please forgive me. I believe the* dvar Torah *you just sent applies to you, because you*

---

203 Leviticus 6:21.

are always looking for new projects and new ways to help Am Yisrael and create a better relationship with Hashem. I respect that and hope that Hashem will give you the strength to continue to do so. Gmar chatimah tovah and love you.

Sukkot

October 18, 2016

Boker tov, Yakov.

I mentioned something over Shabbat which relates to you and your service and is connected to Sukkot.

A kosher sukkah requires two components: the *schach* (thatched roof) and walls. Rav Ariel explains that the *schach* represents the realm of the heavens as it sits above us and protects us from natural elements such as rain and sun, whereas the walls of the sukkah represent the realm of humankind, as they protect us from threats found on the ground, much as a fortress surrounds and protects its soldiers or inhabitants. The walls and *schach* connect the physical realm of man with the spiritual realm of Hashem. The majority of laws of the sukkah have to do with the walls, which signify our need to work earnestly in our world below to construct a partnership with Hashem.

As you enter the sukkah on your base, it is important to remember that as a *chayal* you are constructing the walls of the sukkah which secure the borders of Eretz Yisrael and ensure the protection of Am Yisrael. You are involved in the ultimate partnership with Hashem which will expedite our nation's redemption.

I am glad you took the time to come shopping with me for the *arba minim* (four species of plants used ritually during Sukkot). Please remember that the Chassid who sold them to us asked that you explain the significance of them to the other *chayalim*. These may be the only occasions when many of your fellow *chayalim* will experience these mitzvot.

Chag sameach!

► *The Chassid who sold us the* arba minim *was a nice guy.*
I'll certainly bear in mind what he asked and what you
are saying about demonstrating to my fellow soldiers
the mitzvot, but I also have to be careful not to appear
forceful. Remember, I have to live with these guys and
deal with them every day for a long period of time, and
so I have to be careful not to sound pushy or coercive;
otherwise they will be offended and I could lose my good
standing with them, which I need both theoretically and
practically.

I understand where you are coming from, and you know that I am sensitive to these concerns. That is why I started my organization Makom Meshutaf in the first place. But what I have discovered in my work in Makom Meshutaf is that people are thirsty for knowledge and understanding, particularly if it is presented in the proper way. Your fellow *chayalim* know very well that you are observant, and they are probably familiar with some of the mitzvot that you keep in their company. They are also probably curious to understand what you are doing. Again, you have to tread carefully and offer explanations with the proper sensitivity, such as an intellectual exercise which they might appreciate. If done in the right way, these small experiences and exchanges can affect their lives; most of the time we don't even know.

You know, it's interesting, the Gemara Yerushalmi proposes making a *berachah* on the actual construction of the sukkah: "One who makes a sukkah for himself should recite 'Blessed is He Who has sanctified us with His commandments and has commanded us regarding building a sukkah.'"[204]

We of course do not follow this opinion of the Gemara, because the completion of the mitzvah of the sukkah is actually sitting in it, but what

---

204 Jerusalem Talmud, *Berachot* 9:3.

we should appreciate from the Gemara is the importance placed on doing and constructing, as mentioned above; building something is reason enough to recite a *berachah*. Keep building and constructing in your own way, and with God's help, you too will have reason to recite blessings.

Vezot Haberachah

October 8, 2017

Good morning, Yakov.

Here is something to reflect upon during the ten days of repentance: in Vezot Haberachah it says, "And this for Judah, and he said: Hear, Lord, the voice of Judah, and return him to his people; may his hands fight his grievance, and You shall be a help against his adversaries."[205]

The *pasuk* is the blessing offered to the tribe of Yehudah, but it contains a personal message regarding the path to repentance as well. At first a person asks Hashem to "Hear...the voice of Judah," meaning that Hashem should listen to his prayers and accept his return to Him. When his prayers and repentance are accepted, then he will feel part of the nation of Israel again, and Hashem will "return him to his people" because Hashem is different from mankind, for His "hands fight his grievance." Hashem is able to accept us back regardless of our past behavior, something that man is incapable of doing. Finally, once Hashem accepts the person back, He will also serve as "a help against his adversaries" to assist the person to overcome his inclinations and avoid punishment.

---

205 Deuteronomy 33:7.

The End and the Beginning

January 24, 2018

Good morning, Yakov.

As we are still in the early stages of a new cycle of the *parashiyot* of the Torah, you are now entering the final stages of your service in Tzahal, and I thought this would be appropriate.

When the Torah introduces the mitzvah of being fruitful and multiplying, it says, "And God blessed Noah and his sons, and said to them, 'Be fruitful and multiply, and fill the land.'"[206]

However, when Hashem directs the animals to be fruitful and multiply, He says: "Bring forth with you every living thing that is with you of all flesh, both fowl, and cattle, and every creeping thing that creeps upon the earth, that they may swarm in the earth, and be fruitful, and multiply upon the earth."[207]

Regarding the animals, Hashem says that they should "be fruitful and multiply" to cover the land physically, but in the directive to mankind Hashem adds, "be fruitful and multiply, and fill the land." To "fill the land" means to find purpose in the world and contribute to it in a meaningful way, something that only mankind is capable of doing, and exactly what you are doing through your service.

Glad I had a chance to come by yesterday to the border and treat you guys to pizza and refreshments.

Our lives are supposed to have a reason, and the Torah helps us identify and fulfill that meaning. I saw on someone's WhatsApp picture a saying from Rabbi Nachman of Breslov, which I thought was very meaningful: "The day on which you were born is the day that Hashem decided the world cannot exist without you."

---

206 Genesis 9:1.
207 Genesis 8:17.

Serving in Tzahal was your purpose over the last few years. Always search for purpose in life, and success will follow.

▸ *Thank you for coming by yesterday and treating us to pizza and refreshments. It means a lot to all of us not only in terms of the food (which is great, believe me) but just knowing that someone comes out to see us in the middle of nowhere is pretty inspiring. The guys also enjoyed hearing the* dvar Torah *you gave over, and thanks for keeping it short.*

February 15, 2018

▸ *My dear father,*
Thank you for all of your continued support during the course of my service. I greatly appreciate all you have done for me.
Yakov

The collage Yakov presented to me as a gift at the end of his service

AFTERWORD

It was a cold and rainy Shabbat in January, and the electricity in our home blew during the waning hours of Shabbat. Over the prior few weeks, as I was completing this *sefer*, I had reviewed my WhatsApp communication with Yakov over the past three years, to see if there was anything else I wanted to include or exclude from our correspondence, and now I found myself sitting at home with him on Shabbat in the dark. Reflectively, I mentioned to Yakov how I had reviewed the WhatsApps we exchanged over the past few years while he was serving, and I remarked how impressive it was that by now he had given almost three years of his life to the Israeli army and the Jewish people. He turned to me without pause and said, "It is not enough; I would gladly give more."

With that he informed me that when he finished the army he was going to work in security.

Am Yisrael chai!

ESSAYS RELATING TO ISRAEL AND SERVICE IN TZAHAL

THE CHALLENGES OF JEWISH
IDENTITY IN TZAHAL

I Am My Brother's Keeper

A number of years ago Salon Asyag, whose daughter had been drafted into the IDF, complained that during the first week of her daughter's service, she was taken to Kfar Chabad, where she participated in the *hafrashat challah* ceremony (ritual separation of dough in fulfillment of the requirement in Numbers 15:18–21). Salon was disturbed not only that her daughter had participated in the ceremony but also that the army would advocate such rituals and write them off as educational and cultural experiences. Asyag asserted that the army was guilty of religious coercion; she was troubled by the fact that "one of the first values that my daughter received from the IDF was the value of being a religious Jew; this is not a value I would have expected the Israeli army to give my child."

As a result of Salon's complaints, the ensuing weeks brought with them much scrutiny and skepticism toward the Jewish Identity Branch of the IDF and the work they do with soldiers.

To make matters worse, during that same period, Professor Yagil Levy published a book called *Hamefaked Ha'elyon* in which he criticized army rabbis as being coercive and religious Zionist rabbis for trying to force religion upon the army by sending "too many" of their "fanatical" religious Zionist students to superior combat units. Levi also claims in his book that the rabbis of the IDF transmit subliminal religious messages

217

to commanding officers and soldiers and are intent on spreading radical religious mantra.

Colonel Gershon Hakohen (res.), who is from a religious Zionist family but who is himself not observant, commented that what Levy suggests in his book is utterly ridiculous and that he is merely expressing a fear prevalent among many nonreligious communities throughout Israel. Hakohen explains that these Israelis refuse to recognize that a large part of the Israeli scene today, including the IDF, are religious, or at the very least identify with what religion has to offer. I am not sure I completely agree with him, but I do believe that large segments of the secular Israeli public today are beginning to recognize that in today's day and age, ideology is hard pressed, and the prevailing voice of ideology today in the IDF stems from religious, observant, and traditional soldiers.

Hakohen said, "The group of people that Levy represents [from the left] are decreasing in numbers and becoming weaker, and therefore they delegitimize a group that is growing and becoming more influential, in order to make themselves feel more important or to relieve their concerns." He concluded that "the atmosphere and education that religious Zionist youth receive, be it from school or from the home, are demanding in terms of their encouragement and allegiance to the Jewish land and people, and it is for this reason that students from religious institutions are the ones who are fighting on the front lines; they have something to believe in, and they know what is worth fighting for."

As someone who works for the Jewish Identity Branch of the IDF, I want to clarify that the Israeli Rabbinate of the IDF goes out of its way to ensure that nothing be received as coercive, but at the same time its obligation and job is to infuse our soldiers, regardless of their religious affiliation or lack thereof, with a sense of Jewish identity. Practically this means that we try to provide our soldiers with a sophisticated understanding of the basics and foundations of our heritage. We do so by reviewing certain insights and texts from the Torah, witnessing rituals from

Jewish holidays such as conducting Passover Seders, blowing the shofar on Rosh Hashanah, and hosting Purim parties on base, as well as guiding seminars and trips to places of historical significance in Israel and offering insights about these places both from a traditional as well as a Zionistic perspective. I might add that many lectures and activities are optional, and the ones that are mandatory typically deal with messages of Jewish heroism throughout the ages, including episodes from the Torah and the prophets, as well as Jewish unity and how it is exhibited and can be enhanced in the Jewish homeland.

The Jewish Identity Branch of the IDF is essential to the army because Jewish identity is essential to the existence of the country. This has nothing to do with religion, but it has everything to do with remaining Jewish. Much as America seeks to preserve its patriotic spirit, Israel must sustain its distinctive Jewish character because that is what has ensured our survival – as we have witnessed, often painfully, through the generations. There are many Israelis, including high-ranking officers in the IDF, who either do not recognize this or choose to ignore it. Israel is and always has been a country that is premised upon ideology, and Judaism plays the major role in molding and maintaining that ideology. The upper echelon of the IDF should come to terms with the fact that challah making will not make their soldiers religious, but it may very well fortify their desire to be Jewish, which is the key to a triumphant Israeli army.

IDF Protector of Nations Ideology

As a lecturer for Machane Meshutaf and the Jewish Identity Branch of the IDF, I am often presented with a short window of time during which I am expected to transmit an inspirational message to the soldiers that will hopefully resonate with them after I leave – a message of Jewish unity and pride and the importance of wholeheartedly subscribing to the task at hand, regardless how menial or demoralizing it may seem. Often soldiers are weary and frustrated, little interested in hearing a speech or lecture from me, and so I have to choose my words carefully and use my time efficiently.

I welcome the challenge with reflection and preparation, but when one is confronted with soldiers who are about to experience the danger of engaging in combat, one which I personally never experienced and therefore cannot realistically relate to, one can only struggle to find the correct words to empower and embolden the soldiers to confront their critical objective. In fact, this past week I wrote to a friend of mine in the United States after I had just been on the border trying to help inspire the soldiers, and he wrote back to me that he hoped God would put the right words in my mouth; indeed, I believe that I was able to impart a message to the soldiers, perhaps because God put the right words in my mouth; I share them with you because at this moment of truth for all of us, I believe they will help instill conviction in our hearts as well.

This past week's Torah portion describes the Jewish war effort against the Midianites, sworn enemies of the Jewish nation, during their travels through the desert to reach the land of Canaan (Israel). Interestingly enough, the Torah not only describes the success of the Jewish army but also goes at length to describe the booty, possessions, and wealth that the Jewish people amassed as a result of their victory, which begs the question: why does the Torah describe these spoils of war in such fine detail? Perhaps God wanted to transmit to His people that when one fights for his nation's survival and is willing to sacrifice

for his nation, particularly against a nation that threatens its very existence, indeed there are just rewards for doing so, such as prosperity
and fortune. In stark contrast, when the Jewish people are preparing
to conquer the land of Canaan, they are clearly instructed that they are
not to take from the silver, gold, or any of the consecrated property,
and that it would all go to the treasury of Hashem. Why with regard to
the conquering of Eretz Yisrael were the Jewish people forbidden from
taking the spoils of their war effort?

Conquering and settling the Land of Israel is a holy commandment
from the Torah that is compared to fulfilling all of the commandments
in the Torah itself. God wanted the Jewish nation to appreciate that the
conquest of the Land of Israel and the ability to secure those who wish
to settle it is itself the greatest possible reward one could ask for; in fact,
granting physical reward for such effort would belittle the significance
and wholesomeness of this unique commandment.

Mivtza Tzuk Eitan (Operation Protective Edge), as well as the last
few IDF operations, is not about territory but rather about ideology.
Hamas are well aware that they cannot conquer the Land of Israel from
the people of Israel, but they are interested in disseminating a message of terror and perpetrating acts of chaos, destruction, and murder
throughout Eretz Yisrael; doing so is rewarding for them. In stark contrast, the soldiers of the IDF recognize that their ability to protect the
great nation of Israel and to ensure its safety, to restore order to a land
with so many outstanding accomplishments and so much potential, is
rewarding enough in itself. Soldiers of the IDF do not fight for territory,
nor do they plunder the goods of war; they fight for an ideology committed to promoting productivity and encompassing life.

Recently I was in an air force base which I frequent every week or
so. As I exited my car and approached the *shin-gimel* (base entrance),
a siren sounded. All the soldiers had already made their way to their
shelters, barring the two who were left guarding the *shin-gimel*; I quickly
ducked into the guard station with them. I did not realize that part of

my body was protruding out of the station until suddenly over the loud-speaker one could hear the voice of the commander of the base, saying, "Rabbi, please get back under the shelter and make sure you are entirely inside; after all, you are very important and precious to us."

Our soldiers are fighting for the distinct merit to be able to protect that which is most important and precious to us.

When the Jewish people complete the annual reading of a book within the Torah, all those in the synagogue proclaim, "Be strong! Be strong! And may we be strengthened!"

I no longer struggle for words; to our soldiers I say, be strong, and to the Jewish nation whom they are protecting I say, may we be strengthened by their service and their desire to perpetuate the ideology of this great people.

The Legacy of Our Patriarchs and Matriarchs Is Alive and Well

The entire book of Genesis is full of stories about our patriarchs and matriarchs, describing the impact they had on the people around them and the *kiddush Hashem* they achieved during the course of their productive and challenging lives. Yet as beautiful and inspiring as these stories are, they are nonetheless stories of the past, and it is difficult to imagine people around us in our midst who may fulfill similar callings.

Three weeks ago, our daughter Nechama was drafted into Tzahal. Nechama is an observant young lady, and she knew she was going to be in a unit together with twenty-five nonobservant young women. While she was eager to partake in her unit, she was a bit anxious regarding how things would pan out for her, being the only religiously observant person on her base. The first week after she was drafted was Sukkot, and the *chayalot* (women soldiers) were allowed home for the holiday, but they were told that the first Shabbat back when they returned would be on base, and so they were instructed to prepare accordingly, as they would not be going home for two weeks.

The *chayalot* began to compare notes on their WhatsApp group, texting one another about what they should bring with them to base so that they could all make things a little more enjoyable for their Shabbat together in the army. A number of girls suggested they bring a boom box so they could play music, dance together, and make some noise. Immediately this suggestion was nixed, as a number of *chayalot* reminded the group that Nechama was observant of Shabbat, and it would be unfair that she could not participate and disrespectful of her way of keeping the Shabbat; and so it was agreed that everyone would bring board games so that Nechama could partake. When Nechama told us of this exchange, I told her (tongue in cheek) that she had not even spent that much time with the other *chayalot*, and she already was having a positive influence on her surroundings.

The week passed by, and on Friday Nechama called us from base in an emotional state. She said that she was nervous spending Shabbat on base as the only observant soldier, and she explained that her secular officer sat the *chayalot* in a circle the day before and asked them what Shabbat meant to each of them. Some said that Shabbat was about going to the movies, some said going out to eat, and some just welcomed the chance to sleep. Nechama responded that Shabbat for her was her mother's challah and chicken soup, and with that she was brought to tears and left the room. A few of her comrades came over to her and told her that they understood that she was the only religious girl and reassured her that they would be going to the *beit knesset* (synagogue) with her on Shabbat. When I heard this, I reminded Nechama again of the impact she was having, considering the short amount of time she had been in the army, and I told her that if she was lonely or sad over Shabbat, she should remind herself of the *kiddush Hashem* she was fulfilling through her service.

Motzaei Shabbat (Saturday night), Nechama called and told us the following story. Shabbat morning, she went to the synagogue, and by the time she came back for the Shabbat meal, all of the other *chayalot* were already in the middle of eating. Nechama found some grape juice and approached the table to make Kiddush (the benediction on wine recited on Shabbat) in order to join her fellow soldiers. One of the girls motioned to her to sit down and join them, to which she explained that her *abba* makes Kiddush while standing, so she too would stand for Kiddush. Suddenly, all twenty-five *chayalot* stood up and respectfully remained standing in anticipation of Nechama's Kiddush for Shabbat. Nechama was overwhelmed with emotion and she had to excuse herself and walked out of the dining hall.

The nonobservant officer approached her and told her as follows: "Nechama, there are twenty-five *chayalot* inside who never heard Kiddush in their lives. They are now waiting for you to make Kiddush for Shabbat. Please take this opportunity and recite the Kiddush for our dining room," and so she did.

Yes, my friends, the stories of our forefathers and their lives may have happened long ago, but their memories and the lessons they leave us continue to resonate within us, presenting us with opportunities to fulfill *kiddush Hashem* to this very day.

Memorializing the Living

Both Yom Hashoah and Yom Hazikaron memorialize and beg the question regarding the most appropriate way to commemorate the memories of our Jewish martyrs and heroes. While there are many responses and varied opinions addressing this question, I am certain that effective Judaism is a religion that demands we never forget. Our reflection on the past should invoke a response that helps perpetuate our future. This message has always been and continues to be relevant and vital to our nation's existence, particularly during the times in which we find ourselves.

When the generation following Noah built the Tower of Babel in an attempt to reach the heavens, they were punished for their outright rebellion against God. It is important for us to recognize that historically, all these people knew was failure and destruction: Adam and Chavah's sin resulting in their banishment from Eden, Kayin's murder of his brother which resulted in his nomadic existence, and the inevitable destruction of an entire world during the time of Noach. Consequently, the people who followed Noach's generation feared that they too would be killed; their reaction was to build a monument to serve as a towering tombstone. This entire generation of people decided to demonstrate their presence in the world through the marking of a tombstone.

God destroyed the tower not only as a punishment, but also as a means of transmitting a significant message to the world: too much time was spent on commemoration and no time was spent on generating a productive society. The way to honor a memory is not by erecting a stone, but by establishing building blocks of faith, instituting principles and infusing educational values; this way, not only do we commemorate, but we also celebrate the lives of people even when they are no longer physically present, a message which must remain a mainstay of Judaism but which is unfortunately often lost in our indulgent and self-gratifying world.

In a world that persistently endorses the most effective ways to surge forward, it is difficult to promote reflecting on the past even if that reflection is an integral part of ensuring survival; this has become one of the greatest challenges for the Jewish world today. The question we should ask after Yom Hashoah and as we approach Yom Hazikaron is one packed with serious considerations because it involves not only how to memorialize but also how to infuse and stimulate for the sake of perpetuating Israel's future.

Upon visiting Ben-Gurion's home in Sde Boker, you cannot help but notice the Tanach (Hebrew Bible) on his bedside table with its tattered and worn pages, demonstrative of the fact that Ben-Gurion, hardly sympathetic to religion, read and used the book. Ben-Gurion did not do so out of religious conviction, but he read and studied the Bible because he appreciated the significance of knowing who we were in order to identify what we could become. When Menachem Begin was prime minister, he would frequently hold a Bible class on the weekly Torah portion for his cabinet. He valued the blueprint which demonstrates that identifying our persecutions in the past helps us adopt resilience for the future.

Every year as Yom Hashoah approaches, we come closer to the realization that there are only a handful of survivors left who can offer live testimony and replay the images of the catastrophic history they lived through. Every year as Yom Hazikaron approaches, we must come closer to the realization that there are very few Ben-Gurions and Begins amongst us, and it is our duty to equip our youth and our soldiers with a connection to our past in order that they acquire the drive to fight for our future.

I belong to the Harel division of the Rabbinate of the IDF, a special division that offers lectures and presentations on Jewish history and Jewish tradition to all divisions within the IDF. Why is this division necessary within the ranks of the IDF, an army that should concern itself exclusively with protecting its borders and citizens? The reason is that the IDF is a Jewish army, and there are many soldiers who do not know the three forefathers of the Jewish people and cannot identify the Five Books of Moses. One might insist that these concerns are religious by nature, and as there is no religious coercion in the Israeli army, they are trivial in comparison to the greater task at hand, but the problem is that these same soldiers have no clue who Zev Jabotinsky is, either. When Jewish soldiers are unaware who their founding fathers of the past and the present were, then it is indeed difficult to protect Israel's borders and citizens, for the knowledge of our past advances the resilience of our future.

The more we enrich our children and soldiers with Jewish heritage, the more they will comprehend that they are not fighting to kill; rather, they are struggling for the right to live. They are not engaged in destruction; rather, they are confronted with the challenges of construction. Our ability to educate our generation with these ideals will ensure that we not only honor the past but commence a future.

JEWISH CALENDAR:
HOLIDAY MESSAGES FROM TZAHAL

Rosh Hashanah: Past Reflections and Future Awakenings

Being that Rosh Hashanah is a time to reflect upon the past year in anticipation of the year ahead, here are three thoughts worthy of contemplation which relate directly to the three sections of the Rosh Hashanah service and reveal the three functions of the shofar.

The first segment of the Rosh Hashanah service, called *malchuyot*, from the Hebrew word *malchut* (kingdom), confirms that God is the master of a people and protector of a nation, a concept that secular Israelis are becoming more comfortable with in theory even if it does not translate to practice. Over the past years we have seen a growth in Israelis who are interested in connecting with their traditions and learning about their history even through the observance of certain practices which they consider Jewish cultural experiences.

Today statistics show that over 56 percent of Israelis light Shabbat candles, over 78 percent participate in a Passover Seder, 69 percent maintain kosher homes, 80 percent say that they believe in God, 65 percent confirm that the Torah is the divine book of the Jewish people, 98 percent of Israelis have mezuzot on their door posts, and 92 percent circumcise their male children. Many Israeli Jews have an interest in the place that religion occupies in the State of Israel and in the meaning of a "Jewish state," and for the vast majority it is important to live in Israel as a means of identifying with the Jewish people.

The second section of the Rosh Hashanah service is called *zichronot*, which emphasizes *zachor* (remember); we are encouraged to reflect upon the historical events that impacted our loyalty to God and to one another and inspired our development into a nation. Over these past years, we witnessed the abduction and cold-blooded murder of three innocent young men by Hamas terrorists. We experienced the height of anxiety as we consistently fled to bomb shelters under a barrage of rockets and missiles fired upon cities throughout Israel, fueling the beginnings of a number of operations, including Operation Protective Edge, whose sole objective was to disclose and destroy a vast network of tunnels created by Hamas terrorists for the purpose of perpetrating terror upon civilians in Israel.

Yet Israel was continuously chastised as the aggressor and for its mistreatment of civilians who were unfortunately harmed or killed during the operation. The world's media referred to Israel as inhumane, regardless of the extraordinary efforts made by the IDF to warn civilians ahead of their planned attacks in order to protect their safety, and regardless of the footage which showed Hamas terrorists harboring themselves in schools and hospitals and using children as human shields in order to protect themselves.

In comparison, mass murderer Syrian prime minister Bashar al-Assad was hardly scrutinized for killing thousands of people using chemical weapons and torturing and killing anyone who opposed his dictatorship. Vladimir Putin's aggression on the Ukraine saw over three thousand deaths as innocent civilians were abducted by both Russian and Ukrainian forces on each side, but he was hardly condemned. The IS (also known as ISIS) seized territories throughout Syria and Iraq in an aggressive Jihadist war path to "conquer the Middle East," butchering and beheading thousands of civilians, and then president Obama remained frighteningly unresponsive.

Yet Obama was not hesitant to join Ban Ki-Moon of the UN, who criticized Israel for supposedly failing to do all it can to prevent civilian casualties in Gaza during Israel's missions against Hamas terrorists. The criticism of Israel from around the world was heard loud and clear, and our supposed ally's silence was just as deafening; this opened Pandora's box as anti-Semitic acts ensued. Jews were attacked in France, Australia, England (where statistics show that anti-Semitism has risen an astonishing 400 percent) and even in places that we would have normally considered secure havens for Jews, such as New York and Miami.

The section of *zichronot* on Rosh Hashanah begs us to verify – as we have done in the past – that the world does not see or interpret the events unfolding around our nation the same way that we do, and that history has a nasty habit of repeating itself. Jewish communities throughout the Diaspora, regardless of how comfortable they feel and how at home they believe they are, must take heed of the events unfolding in front of their eyes and recognize that they are strangers in a strange land, temporary guests whose stay will eventually wear thin as it has done consistently in the past, and that the only land where they can truly feel secure is Israel.

Shofarot, the third and final unit of the prayer service, makes reference to the shofar, the ram's horn, which is blown to mark the day of our redemption. It is during this section that we are expected to think about how we can actively facilitate the redemption we eagerly anticipate, something that was made easier for us to envision over the past few years as we have been privy to witness how some *charedim* have begun to enlist in the IDF and national service. Almost two thousand *charedim* have enlisted in the IDF over the past year, mostly in combat units – an increase of 39 percent from past years. In addition, the percentage of *charedim* joining the work force continues to gradually rise, which may explain the findings that with each progressive year the friction between the secular and the religious in Israel seems to be decreasing.

The first function of the shofar was to gather people and unify the nation; such was the case at the foothold of Mount Sinai when the Jewish nation united for the purpose of accepting the Torah. We have been privileged over the course of the years to witness a nation unite, whether for the sake of praying for three young souls or for consoling their families after the truth of their fate was revealed following their abduction. Israelis traveled en masse to the towns bordering Gaza to offer relief and supplies to the residents in the Negev and our soldiers who were protecting them, and thirty thousand people converged for the sake of escorting a lone soldier to his burial place in an effort to console his parents, whom none of the consolers had ever previously met.

The shofar also sounds in order to amass troops and prepare them for war, as was the case with Joshua when he led the Jewish people by the alarm of the shofar to conquer the land of Canaan. This year we have witnessed troops gather from all walks of Jewish life, secular and *charedi* alike, for the sake of protecting the same borders that were defended by David Hamelech before us.

With Rosh Hashanah swiftly approaching, we can proudly declare that we have been privileged to witness and benefit from the first two purposes of the shofar. When Rosh Hashanah arrives, as we crown our king and recount our history, perhaps it is time for us to demand that we witness the third purpose of the shofar come to fruition, in preparation for our redemptive future.

Niko and the IDF Course for Conversion

What are the Yamim Norayim (High Holidays), and what should they mean to us? Pose that question to an observant Israeli Jew, and I imagine he or she will sum it all up with one word, *teshuvah* (repentance); but pose the same question to a secular Israeli, and you are bound to hear something different, such as festival, or apples and honey, or perhaps a new beginning. All the responses are correct, but there is a common thread that encompasses the meaning of the High Holidays and binds us all together.

One of the programs Makom Meshutaf added to our programming is secular pre-military academies. These are attended by secular youth who, prior to their service in the army, opt to spend a year studying their roots, volunteering and embracing an ideology of being a pioneer in Israel so they can appreciate and enhance their army experience even more. Many of the secular pre-military academies do not include Torah study and identifying with Judaism from a (non-coercive) Torah perspective, which is where we come in. Makom Meshutaf now offers *shiurim* (classes or lectures) on Jewish foundations and basics to eleven secular pre-military academies on a consistent basis.

One of the *mechinot* that I frequent is called Asher Ruach Bo (the spirit within), and it is a unique academy. Asher Ruach Bo is for young men who are juvenile delinquents. Many of them have criminal records, and the founder of the academy believes that under different circumstances and in the right environment, these young men can flourish. He made a deal with the courts in Beer Sheva that if we can transform these young men into combat soldiers for the army, the court will clear their criminal records. I am the rabbi at the *mechinah*, the only person who comes to teach at the *mechinah* about Judaism, and through Makom Meshutaf I offer them *shiurim* on Torah and Jewish ethics; otherwise they would get nothing.

The last meeting I had with the students prior to their leaving and moving on to their units in Tzahal, I told them they should be in touch with me whenever and for whatever they need, and I gave them my number.

One of my students from Mechinah Asher Ruach Bo is a young man named Niko who is not Jewish. He opted to do the Netiv conversion course through the army, but he had no support from his parents and very limited connection with them. Through his connection with me at the *mechinah,* he called me and asked if I would serve as his adopted family and teach him about Judaism and Shabbat. During his conversion course, Niko would meet me in shul on Friday night and join us in our home quite often for *seudot Shabbat.* Yet toward the end of the course, I began to hear less from Niko and, while I wondered why he became scarce, I did not want to confront him and cause him to feel uncomfortable, so I decided to give him the breathing space that he may have needed. Nonetheless, I wondered what had become of him and particularly of his quest to become a Jew.

A few months after I had last heard from Niko, I went to speak at the Tzanchanim (Paratroopers) base. I was asked to speak twice, but I was told that there would be an hour window between the two *shiurim,* and if I wanted, I could opt to leave after delivering the first *shiur.* I told my wife, Gabi, that I would probably just stick around to deliver the one *shiur,* to which she advised that I stay for both, as I would find something to do during the hour in between (I suspect she was weighing the advantage of having me out of the house for an extra hour). The first *shiur* was off base in the surrounding fields, and when I returned to the base to wait for my second *shiur,* I noticed that I had received a message from none other than Niko, who asked if I was still in the Tzanchanim base. He reminded me that he was serving in Tzanchanim; if I was on base, he wanted to come speak with me.

When I saw Niko, we gave each other a warm greeting, and he began to explain to me that he was forced to leave the Tzanchanim combat forces for various reasons. He was given a job to monitor who enters and leaves the base. When I arrived at the base, the soldiers at the main gate radioed ahead to the monitoring station asking if a rabbi named Shalom had clearance to enter the base; Niko was the soldier on duty at the station, and he explained to me that he was the one to give the OK for me to come on base because as far as he knew, there was only one rabbi named Shalom who went around speaking on bases. Niko then told me that he ran out of his station and started chasing my car because he wanted to talk to me, but I had not noticed and drove on, at which point he texted me.

He explained that the reason he lost contact with me was that he was not sure now whether he wanted to go through with becoming a Jew, and he did not want me to be disappointed. He said that all the obligations one has as a Jew are burdensome and too restricting, and he was just not sure he could make such a commitment; besides he was unsure where God fit into the entire picture, if at all.

I thanked Niko for making the effort to find me in order to discuss the matter. I then told him that he was always welcome in our home whether he was Jewish or not; but then I told him how Gabi had convinced me to stay for both *shiurim*, and were it not for her having done so, I might not have had the opportunity to meet up with him again. Happenstance? I think not. Was it a coincidence that Niko was in charge of monitoring the base that day and that he happened to be by his station at the very moment they radioed in about my arrival? I was given ample opportunity to explain to Niko that he should not be overwhelmed by the opportunities Judaism has to offer, and that sincere spiritual growth can only be accomplished one step at a time, because at the end of the day all Hashem expects from us is to try to take the next step. While he wasn't completely convinced, Niko was overcome with relief and willing to consider his affiliation with the Jewish people once again.

The Yamim Norayim are about apples and honey, festivals, and family, and they are also about recognizing that for reasons we usually don't understand, we somehow are graced with the encouragement to take a deep breath and start again.

As we concluded our conversation, I asked Niko if he would come join us again next Shabbat. He said that he would, but I was not convinced that he meant it, and so toward the end of the week with admittedly a bit of skepticism, I texted him to find out if he was coming to join us for Shabbat. Without pause Niko texted me back, "Are you kidding me? I've been looking forward to Shabbat at your house the entire week."

Ahhhhhh…to begin again.

A Message for Chanukah to the IDF

I would like to think that most of us in Israel recognize something that our Western democratic allies either do not recognize or choose to ignore because it makes them uncomfortable: the struggles, wars, intifadas, and waves of terror that we confront here in the Jewish State of Israel are not founded upon strategic planning or even military tactics and control, nor are they solvable based on compromise and diplomacy. The volatile confrontations we deal with here are deeply rooted in religion and premised upon our faiths and beliefs. The fact that the Temple Mount continuously finds its way into the heart of the heated contest between both sides is telling enough.

While historically there are always some members in our government who choose to deny this, I believe that the majority of the government and the Israeli public understands this all too well, which is why the solution (one would like to think there is one, even if it does not appear on the immediate horizon) has little if anything to do with negotiations. Arguments and disputes of a spiritual nature cannot be solved and do not manifest themselves through physical means, which is what makes them so challenging in the first place. While I do not have a solution for this issue, I recognize the value of deriving a message that can reinforce our understanding of who we are and what our nation represents, a message that has consistently ensured our survival and is worth reviewing, a religious message which often comes from the most unexpected of places.

Our son Yakov is an observant young man who served in a brigade in the army consisting mainly of nonobservant soldiers. His brigade comprised 121 soldiers, of whom only ten were observant. My wife and I drove to his post one Friday before Shabbat to visit with him and his comrades as they were guarding one of the borders. When we arrived, the staff sergeant, who is not observant, was addressing Yakov's platoon in preparation for Shabbat, which was swiftly approaching. After he reviewed all the security measures and precautions, he concluded his instruction by stating that there was a most crucial issue he wanted to address. He went on to explain how the holy day of Shabbat, the day when religious people rest, would soon begin, and while he understood that the majority of his soldiers did not observe the Shabbat, including himself, it was extremely important to be respectful of those who did.

He asked that soldiers not speak on their cell phones in front of Shabbat observers, that they maintain composure around them, and if a soldier's parents were coming to visit on Shabbat that they too should be careful not to infringe upon the peace and serenity that the observant soldiers sought during the Shabbat day. Finally, he insisted that this post was strictly kosher and that any food brought by parents for their sons on Shabbat should not be brought into the confines of their camp, to ensure that the standards of *kashrut* were maintained out of respect for the observant soldiers and for the soldiers who would assume this position next. The staff sergeant seemed certain that his orders resounded throughout his troops, but I don't think he realized how much those orders penetrated the heart of a bystander. His words reminded me that, while many of my fellow Israelis were not observant, they were Jewish and deeply religious; religiously united, religiously humane, religiously driven by a common nationality and an altruistic cause.

When there are waves of violence in Israel waged by Hamas and Palestinian terrorists, it is undoubtedly frightening, but it would serve us well to remember what we represent and what the perpetrators of terror and violence do not. One outstanding (and disturbing) feature of these recent waves of terror, as many have pointed out, is that the attacks are executed by youth who are easily influenced by the satanic rhetoric emanating from their mosques and the provocative lies emerging from the Palestinian Authority itself. These youths are desperately searching for a calling and longing to believe in something, but unfortunately all that is offered them from their so-called leaders and mentors is violence and chaos, a road that inevitably will lead to their demise.

Abraham, the founding forefather of our nation, realized that there were two components necessary for people to embrace faith in one God: peoplehood and compassion. He consistently invited people to partake of his hospitality, seizing any occasion to engage in theological dialogue and allotting his guests opportunity to become part of a group longing for something constructive and principled. These principles remain the tenets of our faith, as they have in the past, and they will continue to imbue us with resilience regardless of the consistent threats to our existence.

With the arrival of the month of Kislev, Chanukah is upon us. On Chanukah we celebrate the miracle of the oil that lasted for eight days and the victory of the Hasmoneans over the Greek and Syrian dominion in Israel. There is however an additional element to reflect upon during the festival of lights. Nachmanides talks extensively about how the Hasmonean dynasty lost their control of the Jewish nation and their influence in Judea. He explains that the Hasmoneans were priests and not entitled to rule as kings over the Jewish people, a right which belonged exclusively to those from the tribe of Judah. Although there was a temporary need that justified their ascent to the throne, nonetheless they should have returned the glory of kingship back to the tribe of Judah in due course, which they did not do, and their abuse of power lead to family friction, sibling rivalries, and power mongering. Their infighting spawned hatred among the Jewish people, and ultimately the Hasmoneans did to themselves what the Syrians and Greeks could not do.

Our enemy's attempts to wield their weapons and espouse hatred are painful but short-lived, as they have been throughout our arduous history. This coming Chanukah it behooves us to remember what history has taught us consistently – that self-inflicted wounds are often the most fatal and that so long as our modern-day Yehudah the Maccabee can stand up in front of his soldiers, observant and nonobservant alike, and demand that they respect one another, perhaps our salvation will be miraculously revealed once again.

Passover: Free at Last

Every year as we approach Passover, the Jewish holiday that celebrates freedom, I struggle with the same question: What is the definition of freedom and how does it reveal itself in the context of the modern world in which we live today? Deriving a suitable answer can be challenging, yet it is the objective of the entire holiday. On the one hand we are required to reflect upon the enslavement of our ancestors in Egypt, an event that transpired millennia ago and should therefore be foreign to us. On the other hand, it is difficult for us to comprehend freedom in a world that inundates us with pressure and obligations. Perhaps it is for this reason that the Torah obligates us on the Seder night to impart the message of Passover and the Exodus by way of a story. Stories conjure our imagination, encourage dramatic reenactment, and stimulate perspective; and so, in preparation for Passover I would like to share the following personal experiences which I believe will help augment our comprehension of what Judaism calls freedom.

I offer lectures and classes on Judaism to secular kibbutzim and moshavim across the country. A few weeks ago, I contacted a fellow who was in charge of cultural events in the secular moshav, Tzur Natan, regarding my coming by to offer one of my presentations. He told me he was interested and asked me to call him back in a few days to further explore my proposal. When I called him back two days later, the fellow informed me that his mother had just died, and he was thankful that I called because he wanted to fulfill the traditional Jewish laws of mourning, but he was not sure how to do so and was in need of guidance. Bearing in mind that we had briefly spoken on the phone only once before, and had actually never met, he explained he did not know any rabbis and asked if I would assist as his rabbi, to which I obliged.

Two days later I called the man from Tzur Natan to inquire about his welfare. He explained to me that he would be honored if I would deliver a class regarding Jewish unity on the seventh day of mourning, Shushan Purim, to honor the memory of his mother; again, I obliged. And so, this Shushan Purim I did not participate in my family's traditional Purim meal in Jerusalem because I went to Tzur Natan to offer and deliver a message on Jewish unity to a group of secular Jews I was not acquainted with, to honor the memory of a woman I had never met, out of respect for a man I did not know.

The man from Tzur Natan frequently calls me to ask questions and discuss fundamentals of Judaism; I have become his confidant, and last week, after discussing a particular law pertaining to his mourning period, he proclaimed, "Rabbi, I am glad that I have found someone whom I feel comfortable enough to ask my questions. You have helped me achieve freedom."

Freedom from a Jewish perspective is not defined by a person's physical status or financial security; it is a qualitative experience which even someone in mourning, at the height of despair, can access by aspiring toward a more purposeful existence.

This past year I spent a Shabbat in Hispin in attendance at the annual Shabbat with the Jewish Identity Branch of lecturers of the IDF to which I belong. The Jewish Identity Branch of the IDF consists of a group of handpicked lecturers and educators who, regardless of their differences, all share the same objective: to infuse the soldiers with a sense of identity and purpose. Our talks are devoid of anything that might be interpreted as religious coercion or political affiliation. Our words reveal our mission: to remind the soldiers of who they are and what they represent and to inspire them to believe that identifying with their past is key to preserving the Jewish people's future.

I wait in anticipation for this Shabbat because it is the only time during the year, at least that I am aware of, when a most diverse crowd of Chabad Chassidim, other *charedim*, Religious Zionists from the center of the country, *mitnahalim* from the settlements along the West Bank, Sephardim and Ashkenazim, agree to put aside all of their differences and disagreements and congregate for one purpose and with one goal in mind. No one is interested in discussing our differences nor does anyone show any sign of discomfort because of them; quite the contrary, each and every one of us are genuinely concerned with learning from one another and disclosing our successes and failures.

One of the places I visit every week is an army prison in which a number of those imprisoned include *charedi* young men who refuse to serve in an army of a country and a government that they delegitimize. I expressed my frustration to the group over Shabbat about how difficult it was for me to offer a presentation meant to motivate and infuse the same principles of Zionism and idealism which some of these young men rejected in the first place; to me this represented a personal conflict of interest. In response, one of the *charedi* lecturers who was listening to me advised that I should try to see beyond the outer appearances of these young men; after all, he explained, many of them were lost and were just looking for someone or something to give meaning to their lives. He explained that at the end of the day these were young men who needed help, and any hint of inspiration in their lives could potentially encourage them toward a more substantial life.

Here I was being politely told by a *charedi* fellow that I should try to see beyond the periphery and concentrate on the important task at hand. I was reminded that this Shabbat we unite for the sake of furthering the mission of our organization. This one Shabbat our concerns and perspectives were the same. This one Shabbat we would focus upon the soldiers, their ideals, and the awesome contributions they make to help ensure national security, and what we could continue to do to infuse them with the strength to continue to do so. This one Shabbat we would be truly free – free of disparity, free of espousing political alignments, free of casting suspicions. This one Shabbat we would declare that we are free men graced with a shared objective and working toward a common goal.

Jewish freedom is not defined by the man; it is distinguished by an objective and completed with intent. As the maxim erroneously attributed to Jean-Paul Sartre goes, "Freedom is what you do with what's been done to you"; indeed, there is much to be done for the sake of our freedom and much more freedom to be had by all.

Facilitating Redemption

The meaning of freedom is a difficult question considering that one of the definitions of freedom is the absence of subjection to foreign domination or to a despotic government. In a world of impending danger and observable tyranny, how can one contemplate freedom or consider redemption?

Classically, freedom is associated with independence and nonconformity, terms which can be misunderstood as irresponsibility. Judaism however teaches that freedom is rendered through accountability and by committing oneself to a cause and purpose. When the Jews first left Egypt they did not sing, nor did they express gratitude or submit a prayer; seven days later after the parting of the Reed Sea, they burst forth in song in recognition of their deliverance; why did they wait so long? Rabbi Yosef Dov Soloveitchik explains that the people of Israel were delivered from Egypt exclusively by God, "with His strong hand and outstretched arm"; however, at the Reed Sea, the Jews participated with the Almighty in the miracle by jumping in the sea before it began to split. The Jewish people's exceptional joy resulted from their being invited by God to take an active role in this wondrous miracle as they learned that only active participation can help ensure spiritual gratification.

This interpretation helps clarify God's response to Moses at the sea, with the Egyptian army closing in behind them and the storming water in front of them. He says to Moses, "Why do you cry to me? Speak to the Children of Israel, that they go forward."[208] Why did God respond this way to Moses's desperation and the people's panic? Why did He react to Moses's helpless cries by challenging him to enter the sea?

When God commanded Moses to march with the Jewish nation into the sea, He was revealing to them His definition of freedom by

---

208 Exodus 14:15.

preparing them for a relationship with Him. Only the free man can choose to enter a partnership that is sincere and deeply meaningful. To partner with God, we must demonstrate both conviction and the willingness to act. The Almighty did not want Moses or the Jewish people, His partners, to lose this opportunity to reveal His greatness to the world. Therefore, He told Moses, "go forward," as if to say, *take action and proceed, and, as a people, you will be free to sanctify My name while the whole world watches.*

Prior to Yakov's being drafted, I overheard him tell a group of his friends, "It does not matter what you do in the army, even if you are cleaning the toilets with a toothbrush you are doing something productive and contributing to our land and our people."

While I believe he had greater aspirations in the army than cleaning the toilets, I was impressed by his selfless attitude and driven remarks, which revealed a desire to "go forward and sanctify God's name" and eagerly embrace his freedom.

The fundamental value that one must partner and partake in order to establish relevance has always been and continues to be the mainstay of Israel's success and the Jewish nation's freedom.

Days of Remembrance Are Days of Redemption

Yom Hashoah (Holocaust Remembrance Day), Yom Hazikaron (Day of Remembrance for the Fallen Soldiers of Israel and Victims of Terrorism), Yom Ha'atzmaut (Israel Independence Day), and Yom Yerushalayim (Jerusalem Day) are collectively referred to by Religious Zionists as Yemei Hageulah (The Days of Redemption). One can appreciate this application to Yom Ha'atzmaut and Yom Yerushalayim, but it is difficult to understand how Yom Hashoah and Yom Hazikaron could be referred to as redeeming, when they are days marred by the ashes of destruction and replete with haunting memories of the deceased. This is a problem we grapple with every year, and many answers have been proposed. This year I experienced something which I believe will enhance the appropriate response.

According to an opinion in the Talmud, we celebrate the holiday of Sukkot because the Jewish people dwelled in temporary makeshift huts, called sukkot, after they were redeemed by God from Egyptian persecution. This begs the question: Why does that warrant celebration? What was so exceptional about the fact that the Jewish nation dwelled in sukkot? Some commentaries suggest that after all their sufferings, naturally the Jews should never have agreed to live in such exposed crude dwellings in the desert. We would have expected them to insist on more permanent structures where they could feel more secure; yet they agreed to live under such precarious and unstable conditions, demonstrating their sincere faith in God and in His commitment to protect them. This act of faith is cause for celebration, and the same can be said regarding survivors of the Holocaust.

The Jewish people should have lost all hope following the decimation of the Jewish communities throughout Europe by the Nazi regime, and yet, beaten and broken, they were determined and faithful enough to perpetuate their future. Survivors of the concentration camps arrived on the shores of Palestine willing to start a new life in what they believed would be their homeland. They were greeted and handed guns, and they were instructed to fight for the establishment of the State of Israel. Any other people would have raised their hands in defeat, insisting that they were too weak and too frail to contemplate such action, and yet they seized the guns and fought for their nation and land. In the Sgula cemetery in Petach Tikva, there are a number of graves marked anonymous; these are believed to be the graves of Holocaust survivors who had no time to submit their own names and left no survivors by which to immortalize their families, and while this fact is gravely disheartening, it is precisely the reason that Yom Hashoah and Yom Hazikaron are included in Yemei Hageulah.

Redemption can be defined as the act of making something better or more acceptable. While there is no question the wounds of Jewish families who lost loved ones during the Holocaust or defending the borders of Israel could never be healed, survivors and settlers alike claimed that they could make things better. Their resilience and faithfulness to the furtherance of the Jewish people would signify that all of their losses were not for naught; I have been privileged to see their spirit survive and their message resonate. Part of redemption, as defined above, is not only about making something better but also making something more acceptable.

A few years ago, I was privileged to see this part of redemption come to fruition. I had gone to speak at the Givati combat base. I was told to make my way to a base in Har Keren to address a group of soldiers from the Tomer Company which I had never heard of. I arrived in Har Keren and was amazed to find aluminum walls surrounding a particular area in the middle of the base. The Tomer Company, which was established in 2014, consists of young men from completely *charedi* homes, some of whom sport long sidelocks and beards, who have decided that they want to serve in the Israeli army under two conditions: The first condition is that they wish to preserve their *charedi* lifestyle as much as possible even while serving in the army; hence, the fenced-off area.

Tomer Company goes through all the same maneuvers and training exercises as any other Givati soldier, but they do so privately within their own division and behind closed quarters. There are no women allowed in their area, they maintain their own kitchen and standards of *kashrut* supervision, and their commanding officers are observant without exception. Most impressive, however, is their second condition, and that is that they refuse to be pencil pushers; if they serve in the army, they insist on being regular combat soldiers and serving in combat units. After my speech I conversed with many of the soldiers, and I was astounded to find many of them were ostracized or on the verge of being excommunicated by their *charedi* communities, some by their own families for serving in the army, yet they maintained that they were doing the right thing and were prepared to suffer the consequences at their private home for the sake of protecting the national home.

That same year I was called to Yad La-Shiryon in Latrun to speak to the second group of new recruits from the Tomer Company on Yom Hashoah. When I walked in to address the soldiers, all of them without exception stood up for me when I entered the room and then proceeded to take out their notebooks to write notes regarding the lecture and Torah class I was about to deliver. Here I was, a clean-shaven Religious Zionist rabbi, shown the utmost respect by *charedi* young men who were reared in communities that never recognized the legitimacy of the State of Israel, and this is what I told them:

> The Jewish people were delivered from Egypt by God, but when they got to the Reed Sea, the sea did not part until a man called Nachshon Ben Aminadav jumped in, and as more and more people took the plunge, the sea continued to split in their merit. The message resounds loud and clear: God wanted the Jewish people to understand that He would not accommodate miracles on His own, but He expected the Jewish people to initiate miracles together with Him. He expected that regardless of the obstructions

we would encounter to our existence throughout our history, we would not fear following Him into the sea or onto the plains of the desert, we would not desist from taking arms for the future of Israel regardless of how downtrodden we are or how much personal aggravation it may cause. These are the truths and faiths that define redemption; they inspired Holocaust survivors to make something better, and they encourage *charedi* young men to make things more acceptable.

Perhaps redemption is not too far off after all.

PERSONAL PERSPECTIVES
AND INSIGHTS

Putting Things into Perspective

Many of us are familiar with the story of the spies who were sent forward by Moshe to scout out and assess the situation in the land of Canaan to facilitate the conquest of Canaan. The undertaking assigned by Moshe to the leaders of the tribes of Israel ended with the majority of them – as well as a large portion of Am Yisrael – being punished and killed by Hashem. Yet identifying what exactly the leaders did wrong and why they were deserving of such punishment when they returned and reported what they saw in Canaan is the subject of much debate and discourse among the commentaries. I suggest that identifying the sin of the spies begins with understanding the instructions that Moshe gave them to begin with. Moshe instructed, "Get you up here into the South, and go up into the mountains; and see the land, what it is; and the people that dwell therein, whether they are strong or weak, whether they are few or many; and what the land is that they dwell in, whether it is good or bad; and what cities they are that they dwell in, whether in camps, or in strongholds; and what the land is, whether it is fat or lean, whether there is wood therein, or not. And be you of good courage, and bring of the fruit of the land."[209]

There is no doubt that Moshe wanted the spies to conduct a thorough investigation of the land and its surroundings; after all, that is the

---

209 Numbers 13:17–20.

only responsible way to assess exactly how they were going to conquer it and fight the seven nations who inhabit it. However, prior to the specifics of the mission, Moshe told them that he wanted them to "see the land, what it is." This English translation does not do justice to the Hebrew text, because the Hebrew words Moshe used were "*ma hi*," which can also mean "what it can be." Moshe knew very well that the leaders of the tribes would inevitably see many disturbing things and they would witness many potentially discouraging challenges, but that is precisely why he asked them to "see the land, [for] what it can be"; he wanted them to see beyond the here and now. He wanted them to be visionaries and to relate to Bnei Yisrael that although there are difficulties, they should remember the great spiritual potential that emanates from Hashem's promised land; but these leaders were incapable of doing so. In fact, when they return from their mission, the Torah says, "They reported to him and said, 'We arrived at the land to which you sent us, and indeed it flows with milk and honey, and this is its fruit.'"[210]

The moment they proclaimed to Moshe and to all of Am Yisrael "this is its fruit" is the moment they demonstrated that they could only see the fruit in front of them, but they were incapable of dealing with a potential that could eventuate with patience and time. To conquer and inherit Eretz Yisrael, one must envision its potential – only then does it begin to make sense and can the dream become a reality.

Perhaps this is why the *parashah* of Shelach ends with the mitzvah of the *techelet* – royal blue, which is the color of one of the strands of the tzitzit. The Talmud says regarding this color, "Why is the color blue [worn on the fringes of a four-cornered garment] so special? For it is a similar color to the sea, and the sea is a similar color to the sky, and the sky is a similar color to the sapphire stone which adorns the throne of the Almighty."[211]

---

210 Numbers 13:27.
211 Babylonian Talmud, *Menachot* 43b.

Rav Avigdor Nebenzahl offers a fantastic insight regarding the comparison of the blue of the tzitzit to the blue of the sea. Most people say that the color of the sea is blue, when in fact it is not – it is actually colorless, but the reflection of the sun makes it appear blue. Rav Nebenzahl explains that there are some people who look at the blue of the tzitzit and to them it is colorless; they are not moved or inspired toward greater commitment. There are some people who look at the tzitzit and indeed, they see blue like the sea; they are inspired, and they see opportunity to strengthen their rapport with Hashem. It is quite appropriate that the mitzvah of blue in the tzitzit concludes the *parashah* of the spies, reminding us that everything in life is a matter of perspective.

As *chayalei Tzahal*, during the course of your training and service there will be many times when you ask yourselves why you are expected to make sacrifices. You may feel that it is unfair that you have to confront such awesome responsibilities and hardships, but as leaders of Am Yisrael you are expected to view things with proper perspective. You are privileged to protect the flag of Eretz Yisrael which bears blue and white, the colors of the tzitzit, and your mission secures a demanding but promising future.

Time to "Speak Peaceably" and "See the Light"

Many of us are familiar with the story of Joseph and his brothers, the jealousy and even hatred that existed between them, and the catastrophic consequences that ensued as a result of that hatred. The Torah describes the brothers' hatred toward Yosef as "they hated him; and they could not speak peaceably to him."[212]

Obviously those who hate someone will not be able to speak to him peaceably; in fact, they would not be able to speak to him at all. The Torah is coming to reveal to us the formula for success in any relationship: it all begins with communication. There was a breakdown in communication within the family of Yakov (which probably knew earlier roots). Yakov did not converse with his ten sons as much as he communicated with Yosef. The brothers, in turn, did not speak that much with their father and certainly not with Yosef, and we all know the outcome. Communicating is not only about talking, it's about knowing how to "speak peaceably." To "speak peaceably" means to employ proper tone and intonation. To "speak peaceably" means to incorporate patience, understanding, and consideration. Most importantly, to "speak peaceably" means to listen attentively.

Perhaps Yakov did speak with his sons, but he did not "speak peaceably"; he probably did not have heart-to-heart conversations with them to appreciate each one of their personalities and accentuate their strengths. In fact, it appears he only did this on his death bed, when he offered each son a blessing in accordance with his unique personality. What Yakov did immediately prior to his death does not appear to be something he did while he was living. Perhaps the brothers and Yosef did speak to one another, but they did not "speak peaceably"; they did not enjoy a comradery as many brothers do, and they did not seek to understand each other's feelings, as they were uninterested in preserving

---

212 Genesis 37:4.

a familial relationship. I often speak to people about why their kids left religion, and while I don't have the answers, I know that it is crucial that the parents stay in touch and communicate with their kids.

Unfortunately our history has a nasty habit of repeating itself. The organization I started in 2014, Makom Meshutaf, offers Jewish programming without a religious agenda to secular kibbutzim and moshavim throughout the country. I guess you could say that Makom Meshutaf bridges gaps and creates initiatives. We ran a panel in Kibbutz Tzora that consisted of a secular Israeli, Religious Zionist (me), and a *charedi* woman. It was a fascinating program and something we are promoting in kibbutzim throughout the country to demonstrate that there are differences between all of us, which is precisely why we need to engage in dialogue. The secular Israeli we invited came with blatant negativity toward our beliefs and a bitter attitude; it was very upsetting. While I understand that everyone has varied perspectives, we have to at least be able to "speak peaceably" and show respect for others' opinions. In fact, the *charedi* woman seemed to have been accepted the most from the *chevrah*, and I think this explains many things. The moment people see someone exhibiting tolerance and the security to listen to others, they are willing to accept as well, and this is what happened.

I once tried to speak with someone from a kibbutz who is in charge of its cultural programming, and he would not even grant me the time of day. As I began my explanation of what we are trying to do, he stopped me abruptly, told me not to call him again, and hung up the phone – an obvious failure to "speak peaceably" and listen.

Our *chayelet* daughter Nechama, the only religiously observant girl in her unit, told me that as part of her course they have an exam every week, and her commanding officer puts a random bonus question on the exam as well. One week the bonus question was to write down the words to the song "Echad Mi Yodea" (Who Knows One?) from the Pesach Haggadah. Sadly, Nechama was the only one who got the bonus question correct. Yet following the exam, naturally all the *chayalot* came to ask Nechama what the bonus question answer was, and she ended up teaching them the entire "Echad Mi Yodea" song, which has now become the "theme song" of their unit. Only when we "speak peaceably" can we hope to reveal to others that they too know the answer to "Who Knows One?"

This week Nechama's sergeant had a heart-to-heart with each soldier privately. Nechama expressed to her that she was a bit disappointed in the lack of motivation at times by some of the girls. Her non-observant sergeant responded, "Remember, Nechama, all the girls who are here are not observant, which means that they have to serve in the army; they don't necessarily want to be here. You on the other hand are observant, you had other options to choose from other than the army, but you chose to be here. Between you and me, as an observant girl you are more motivated because you have something to believe in. It is this belief which provides you with resilience and a strength that other people don't have." Only those who "speak peaceably" can reveal to others that they too know the answer to "Who Knows One?"

Later in the *parashah* we come across the second vital statement as Yakov sends Yosef off to see his brothers, saying, "Go now, see whether it is well with your brothers…"[213]

Yakov is not sending Yosef merely as a messenger, he is sending Yosef as an ambassador of peace; he now sends him to "speak peaceably" to his brothers after all the ill will that festered between them. He asks Yosef to "see whether it is well with" his brothers by seeing them in a more positive light, but it is too late.

Perhaps it would do us well to put aside our differences and learn to "speak peaceably" to one another. Perhaps it is time for us to recognize that our resilience and strength stems from our ability to "see whether it is well with [our] brothers"; those brothers of our past did not do a very good job at it, but it seems that the sisters of our present are doing a fine job indeed.

---

213 Genesis 37:14.

Parah Adumah and the Pre-Military Academy

I wrote the following *dvar Torah* to Yakov in the army during the initial period when my student Niko from Mechinah Asher Ruach Bo was spending time with my family on Shabbat.

Parashat Chukat begins with the mitzvah of the Parah Adumah (Red Heifer), which is very difficult to understand. Even Shlomo Hamelech in his infinite wisdom could not fathom why those Kohanim who are in a state of purity become impure during the process of purifying someone who is *tamei met* (impure through contact with a deceased).

Perhaps the Torah wanted us to comprehend the humanity of it all and to appreciate the potential that exists in each and every one of us. The complex laws of the Parah Adumah remind us of a very simple foundation: even the saintly Kohen Gadol can easily become impure, and even someone as "lost" as a *tamei met* can purify himself if he so desires.

The impact we can have on one another is awesome when we follow the doctrine of Hashem, including of course those directives that seem incomprehensible.

Last night I got the following text from Niko:

> Hi, Rav Shalom, how are you? How is the family? Please send them my best.
>
> I needed to tell you the following. You remember we learned together on Shabbat why the order of "honor your father and mother" is father first and mother second? Well, today in our conversion course this question was posed, and I was able to answer the question from what we learned! I just wanted u to know how much I learn from the Shabbatot I spend at your home. It is truly unbelievable!

I am sending you this not only because you have met Niko a number of times but more importantly because I want you to know that you can never underestimate the effect you can have on people; we have the potential to touch a sensitive chord and to affect even people who seem "lost" spiritually, perhaps even to change the direction of their lives (rarely do we know about it).

You serve together with many secular nonobservant soldiers; they see the kippah on your head, they know that you are granted extra time to get ready in the morning for the sake of *tefillah*, and they witness the way you observe Shabbat as a day to serve and not just to relax. You have been granted a wondrous opportunity to "purify" others by way of example, but you must first recognize that it begins with yourself and your adherence to what we know is true and devout.

If you remember this and embrace the missions in front of you, both the physical ones and of course the spiritual, then one day some of your fellow *chayalim* may reflect upon the "religious observant sergeant" who served in their command, and they too might find themselves saying, "it was truly unbelievable."

Protection and Unification: My Shabbat with Givati Brigade

The Hesder yeshiva program has received criticism for the shorter terms of duty served by its soldiers as they combine Torah study with military service. It is claimed by some that the Hesder soldiers receive preferential treatment.

Sure, there are secular soldiers who continue to resent the fact that Hesder students have a shorter tour of active duty (even though the entire five years that students are part of the Hesder program, they are under the auspices of the army and can be called up for a mission at any time during those years), but there are also many who have tremendous respect for the Hesder students' commitment to both the Torah's directives and to those of the army as well. This respect is mutual, as there are many yeshivot Hesder today that encourage their students to serve in mixed units together with secular soldiers, active-ly promoting tolerance while simultaneously sanctifying the name of Hashem by way of their exemplary behavior and wholehearted com-mitment to Eretz Yisrael and Am Yisrael. Indeed, the one place where there is coexistence and a sense of harmony in Israeli society today is in the army.

I was privileged to deliver a *shiur* to a group of Hesder students temporarily stationed in the middle of the Judean Desert (i.e., in the middle of nowhere). Their assignment was to guard the combat gear and equipment of a commando unit while the commandos were conducting maneuvers, hardly a glorious mission. The camp where the young men are stationed has no generator, and there is no electricity. The last two Shabbatot were spent in the dark – hardly pleasant conditions. Yet the army assigns Hesder students to these types of missions considering the shorter time they are serving and the fact that Hesder students are gen-erally cooperative, another example of the collaboration that can exist between the army and its religiously observant soldiers.

The contribution the Hesder student makes cannot be measured quantitatively. The main voice of Zionist ideology in Israel today resounds from the halls of the Hesder yeshivot, because they infuse faith through the study of Torah and breed soldiers with resolve and purpose. These qualities guarantee the future of the Jewish homeland and the perpetuation of a unified Jewish people.

I strongly believe there is no greater impetus and model for Jewish unity and comradeship than the army. I spent a Shabbat down south on the Givati army base with a group of *beinishim* (acronym for *bnei yeshivot*, i.e., combat units consisting of Hesder yeshiva students) undergoing basic training,

Considering the diversity that exists within the observant Jewish community in Israel today, typically in every city there are Sephardic synagogues and Ashkenazi synagogues, each conducting their respective services separately in accordance with their own liturgy. Classically, it would be very difficult to find a combination of Sephardic and Ashkenazic *nusach* (prayer format) combined within one service; in fact, the closest one would get to such an arrangement is within certain synagogues that offer the option of praying according to each respective tradition under one building but in completely separate rooms.

The only existing institution that offers the traditional Sephardic and Ashkenazic prayers combined and conducted in one synagogue and within the same service and setting is in the army. This miraculous feat is accomplished through mutual respect, a concept which unfortunately has become archaic and foreign to the Jewish community. In 1963 Rabbi Shlomo Goren, the chief rabbi of the IDF, introduced a format of prayer called Achid, from the word *echad* (one), which he hoped would accommodate both Sephardic and Ashkenazic tradition by combining a mixture of both traditions within one service. The format was never fully accepted and did not enjoy widespread popularity, yet the message of what Rabbi Goren was trying to accomplish was clear: togetherness by way of a united prayer, particularly within the framework of the army, where comradeship is so vital.

Today the Hesder yeshiva students serving in the IDF have adopted a different system, which, although it does not follow Rabbi Goren's format, certainly aspires to his ideal. The system can be compared to a tag team by which the Sephardim and Ashkenazim switch off within the same synagogue. The Sephardic prayer format is implemented for the morning service, then the Ashkenazic prayer format is implemented for the afternoon services, then back to the Sephardic tradition for the evening services, and so on and so forth. This system has never been officially introduced or endorsed by the IDF Rabbinate; it is implemented by the yeshiva students and soldiers who, by taking turns, demonstrate solidarity and respect for the traditions and customs of others. They profess that if they can train, fight, and sweat together, then they can certainly pray together as well.

Over Shabbat the solidarity was infectious. Friday night following Shabbat prayers as the guest rabbi, I was asked to recite the Kiddush benediction over the wine. It was now 9 p.m., and the soldiers present were hungry and clearly exhausted from a long week of training, yet prior to my reciting the Kiddush, a number of the Hesder students asked me to wait, as many of the nonobservant soldiers who had not attended the synagogue services and therefore were unaware that we had completed services had not yet arrived to the dining hall. The students explained that it was only appropriate to offer the opportunity for all soldiers to partake from the Shabbat meal together and to hear the Kiddush in unison. I was astounded not only by the consideration of the Hesder boys toward their nonobservant peers, but also by the willingness of the nonobservant soldiers to abstain from eating until the observant soldiers had completed their Friday night services.

Shabbat day in the middle of the desert the temperatures reached a scorching 45 degrees. The *chayalim* were on intense 2:4 guard duty (two hours on, four hours off) for the entire week, and their quarters were outdoors in terribly uncomfortable conditions. I on the other hand was given an officer's room to sleep in over Shabbat which came equipped with an air conditioning unit, and I felt obliged to offer the *chayalim* to nap for a few hours in my room and relieve themselves of the heat, to which they responded, "As much as we realize it would help us rest, we cannot accept your offer, Rabbi, as it would be unfair and inconsiderate to the rest of our unit who are left sleeping outside." While I felt bad that my students would be deprived of an opportunity to get some rest, I was proud that they valued empathy.

Saturday night when Shabbat ended, I went to the officers' quarters to discuss some of the soldiers I knew and their progress. As I approached I noticed that two of the young commanders who were not observant were involved in a heated debate. They asked me if I could be of assistance as they explained that they were discussing whether or not it is acceptable to require the *beinishim* under their command to check if the army radio at their guard stations was working, on Shabbat. One felt that it was not necessary, and therefore he would not require his soldiers to do so, while the other felt that checking the radio fell into the category of *pikuach nefesh* (preserving life in a potentially life-threatening situation) and therefore necessary on Shabbat as well. Not only was I impressed by the obvious concern for safety shown by these commanders, but I was struck by the avid respect they showed for the traditions and laws of the Torah and in turn for their soldiers, the *beinishim*.

The rabbis explain that one of the causes for the destruction of the Temple was *sinat chinam*, unwarranted hatred and intolerance for one another. I strongly believe there is no greater impetus and model for Jewish unity and comradeship than the army.

PRAYER FOR MEMBERS OF THE ISRAEL DEFENSE FORCES
תפילה לשלום חיילי צה"ל

He Who blessed our forefathers
מִי שֶׁבֵּרַךְ אֲבוֹתֵינוּ

Abraham, Isaac, and Jacob,
אַבְרָהָם יִצְחָק וְיַעֲקֹב,

may He bless the fighters of the Israel Defense Forces
הוּא יְבָרֵךְ אֶת חַיָּלֵי צְבָא הַהֲגָנָה לְיִשְׂרָאֵל

and security forces,
וְאַנְשֵׁי כֹחוֹת הַבִּטָּחוֹן,

who stand guard over our land and the cities of our God
הָעוֹמְדִים עַל מִשְׁמַר אַרְצֵנוּ וְעָרֵי אֱלֹהֵינוּ,

from the border of the Lebanon to the desert of Egypt,
מִגְּבוּל הַלְּבָנוֹן וְעַד מִדְבַּר מִצְרַיִם,

and from the Great Sea to the approach of the Aravah,
וּמִן הַיָּם הַגָּדוֹל עַד לְבוֹא הָעֲרָבָה,

on the land, in the air, and on the sea.
בַּיַּבָּשָׁה בָּאֲוִיר וּבַיָּם.

May Hashem cause the enemies who rise up against us
יִתֵּן יְיָ אֶת אוֹיְבֵינוּ הַקָּמִים עָלֵינוּ

to be struck down before them.
נִגָּפִים לִפְנֵיהֶם!

May the Holy One, Blessed is He, preserve and rescue
הַקָּדוֹשׁ בָּרוּךְ הוּא יִשְׁמֹר וְיַצִּיל אֶת חַיָּלֵינוּ

our fighting men from every trouble and distress
מִכָּל צָרָה וְצוּקָה,

and from every plague and illness,
וּמִכָּל נֶגַע וּמַחֲלָה,

and may He send blessing and success
וְיִשְׁלַח בְּרָכָה וְהַצְלָחָה

in their every endeavor.
בְּכָל מַעֲשֵׂה יְדֵיהֶם.

May He lead our enemies under their sway,
יַדְבֵּר שׂוֹנְאֵינוּ תַּחְתֵּיהֶם,

and may He grant them salvation
וִיעַטְרֵם בְּכֶתֶר יְשׁוּעָה

and crown them with victory.
וּבַעֲטֶרֶת נִצָּחוֹן.

And may there be fulfilled for them the verse
וִיקֻיַּם בָּהֶם הַכָּתוּב

(Deuteronomy 20:4)
(דברים כ,ד)

"For it is the Lord, your God, Who goes with you
"כִּי יְיָ אֱלֹהֵיכֶם הַהֹלֵךְ עִמָּכֶם,

to fight for you against your enemies,
לְהִלָּחֵם לָכֶם עִם אֹיְבֵיכֶם

to save you."
לְהוֹשִׁיעַ אֶתְכֶם".

Now let us respond: Amen.
וְנֹאמַר: "אָמֵן".

PRAYER FOR THE STATE OF ISRAEL
תפילה לשלום המדינה

Our Father in Heaven,	אָבִינוּ שֶׁבַּשָּׁמַיִם,
Rock and Redeemer of Israel,	צוּר יִשְׂרָאֵל וְגוֹאֲלוֹ,
bless the State of Israel,	בָּרֵךְ אֶת מְדִינַת יִשְׂרָאֵל,
the first manifestation of our redemption.	רֵאשִׁית צְמִיחַת גְּאֻלָּתֵנוּ.
Shield it with Your lovingkindness,	הָגֵן עָלֶיהָ בְּאֶבְרַת חַסְדֶּךָ,
envelop it in Your peace,	וּפְרֹשׂ עָלֶיהָ סֻכַּת שְׁלוֹמֶךָ,
and bestow Your light and truth upon its leaders,	וּשְׁלַח אוֹרְךָ וַאֲמִתְּךָ לְרָאשֶׁיהָ,
ministers, and advisors,	שָׂרֶיהָ וְיוֹעֲצֶיהָ,
and grace them with Your good counsel.	וְתַקְּנֵם בְּעֵצָה טוֹבָה מִלְּפָנֶיךָ.
Strengthen the hands of those who defend our holy land,	חַזֵּק אֶת יְדֵי מְגִנֵּי אֶרֶץ קָדְשֵׁנוּ,
grant them deliverance,	וְהַנְחִילֵם אֱלֹהֵינוּ יְשׁוּעָה
and adorn them in a mantle of victory.	וַעֲטֶרֶת נִצָּחוֹן תְּעַטְּרֵם,
Ordain peace in the land	וְנָתַתָּ שָׁלוֹם בָּאָרֶץ,
and grant its inhabitants eternal happiness.	וְשִׂמְחַת עוֹלָם לְיוֹשְׁבֶיהָ.
And gather all the brothers of the house of Israel	וְאֶת אַחֵינוּ כָּל בֵּית יִשְׂרָאֵל,
who are scattered in all the lands	פְּקָד נָא בְּכָל אַרְצוֹת פְּזוּרֵיהֶם,
and lead them, swiftly and upright, to Your city Zion	וְתוֹלִיכֵם מְהֵרָה קוֹמְמִיּוּת לְצִיּוֹן עִירֶךָ
and to Jerusalem, the abode of Your Name,	וְלִירוּשָׁלַיִם מִשְׁכַּן שְׁמֶךָ,
as is written in the Torah of Your servant Moses	כַּכָּתוּב בְּתוֹרַת מֹשֶׁה עַבְדֶּךָ
(Deuteronomy 30:4–6):	(דברים ל,ד-ו):
"If any of yours are dispersed at the ends of the world,	"אִם יִהְיֶה נִדַּחֲךָ בִּקְצֵה הַשָּׁמָיִם,
from there the Lord your God will gather you,	מִשָּׁם יְקַבֶּצְךָ יְיָ אֱלֹהֶיךָ
and from there He will fetch you.	וּמִשָּׁם יִקָּחֶךָ.
And the Lord your God will bring you to the land	וֶהֱבִיאֲךָ יְיָ אֱלֹהֶיךָ אֶל הָאָרֶץ
that your fathers possessed, and you shall possess it;	אֲשֶׁר יָרְשׁוּ אֲבֹתֶיךָ וִירִשְׁתָּהּ,
and He will make you more prosperous	וְהֵיטִבְךָ
and more numerous than your fathers"	וְהִרְבְּךָ מֵאֲבֹתֶיךָ."

And the Lord your God will circumcise your heart,
and the hearts of your children,
to love the Lord your God with all your heart,
and with all your soul
that you may live."
Draw our hearts together to revere
and venerate Your name
and to observe all the precepts of Your Torah,
and send us quickly the Messiah son of David,
agent of Your vindication,
to redeem those who await Your deliverance.
Manifest yourself in the splendor of Your boldness
before the eyes of all inhabitants of Your world,
and may everyone endowed with a soul affirm:
the Lord, God of Israel, is King
and His dominion is absolute."
Amen forevermore.

וּמָל יְיָ אֱלֹהֶיךָ אֶת לְבָבְךָ
וְאֶת לְבַב זַרְעֶךָ,
לְאַהֲבָה אֶת יְיָ אֱלֹהֶיךָ בְּכָל לְבָבְךָ
וּבְכָל נַפְשֶׁךָ,
לְמַעַן חַיֶּיךָ."
וְיַחֵד לְבָבֵנוּ לְאַהֲבָה
וּלְיִרְאָה אֶת שְׁמֶךָ,
וְלִשְׁמֹר אֶת כָּל דִּבְרֵי תּוֹרָתֶךָ,
וּשְׁלַח לָנוּ מְהֵרָה בֶּן דָּוִד
מְשִׁיחַ צִדְקֶךָ,
לִפְדּוֹת מְחַכֵּי קֵץ יְשׁוּעָתֶךָ.
הוֹפַע בַּהֲדַר גְּאוֹן עֻזֶּךָ
עַל כָּל יוֹשְׁבֵי תֵבֵל אַרְצֶךָ,
וְיֹאמַר כֹּל אֲשֶׁר נְשָׁמָה בְּאַפּוֹ:
"יְיָ אֱלֹהֵי יִשְׂרָאֵל מֶלֶךְ,
וּמַלְכוּתוֹ בַּכֹּל מָשָׁלָה!"
אָמֵן סֶלָה.

265